TITUS ANDRONICUS

TITUS ANDRONICUS

William Shakespeare

WORDSWORTH CLASSICS

This edition published 1996
by Wordsworth Editions Limited
Cumberland House, Crib Street, Ware,
Hertfordshire SG12 9ET

ISBN 1 85326 290 0

*Printed and bound in Great Britain
by Mackays of Chatham plc, Chatham, Kent*

INTRODUCTION

Titus Andronicus was long suspected of being a play of composite authorship, but scholars now generally concede that it is one of Shakespeare's earliest works, and probably his first tragedy. It seems to have been written circa 1589 and appeared in the Quarto of 1594 and the First Folio of 1623. Enormously popular with Elizabethan audiences, it has been disregarded since the time of James I, but interest in the play has recently revived and has commanded recognition of its qualities.

The story of Titus Andronicus is not related to any known events in Roman history, but derives from a variety of classical sources, the chief of these being Seneca's *Thyestes* and Ovid's *Procne and Philomela*. Set approximately in the 4th century AD, its broad political theme illuminates the destructive repercussions of civil war. The macabre plot concerns the revenge of Roman conqueror Titus Andronicus on Tamora, Queen of the Goths, for the atrocities she commits against his family. The fashionable theme of revenge is played out with much violence and melodrama against the decadence of Imperial Rome in its decline.

The play which presents human sacrifice, rape, torture, mutilation, decapitation, cannibalism and murder and leaves fewer than half its characters living, has been defended as a political allegory. Shakespeare's cool, detached treatment of the carnage is notable and conveys a certain sense of moral disgust. In Shakespeare's time, political order and moral order were inextricably connected, and although the crude barbarism embodied by Aaron and Tamora is obviously contrasted with the relatively decent values of Titus and of Rome, a city referred to as 'but a wilderness of tigers', it is clearly no longer the exemplary civilization that it was.

Titus Andronicus is invariably measured against the plays of Shakespeare's maturity, and in this light its structure has been severely and unjustly criticized. Its planning seems masterly when compared with the work of other dramatists of its day. The action is episodic and the play has a series of climaxes rather than culminatiing in a single major scene, and yet it retains a sense of organic identity. At the time that it was written, much drama derived from non-dramatic verse which perhaps accounts for the tendency of characters in *Titus Andronicus* to address the audience rather than each other. Despite this there are some brilliant speeches, some lyrical passages where imagery is effectively deployed, and humour too in the sardonic wit of the villain Aaron. The play abounds with promise, foreshadowing Shakespeare's later great tragedies in many ways.

Titus himself is a flawed character who lacks the conventional qualities of a tragic hero yet is peculiarly interesting for his affinities with later heroes such as Lear, Othello and even Hamlet. Like Lear, Titus' implacability clouds his judgement, leading him to violent crime, and to madness both feigned and unfeigned (which also foreshadows Hamlet). Like Coriolanus, another of Shakespeare's Romans, Titus never achieves redemption through self-knowledge, but this is precluded by the very nature of revenge tragedy. Titus' prowess and decisiveness as a commander of men on the battlefield contrasts sharply with his helplessness in the hands of demonic civilian schemers, presaging the manipulation, bewilderment and isolation of Othello. The villainous Aaron has elements of Iago, and his relationship with Tamora forms a sub-plot to the main action which looks forward to sinister intrigues in later works, particularly *King Lear*.

Titus Andronicus, for all its faults is a challenging play conceived on a grand scale, superior in design and execution to most contemporaneous drama. For all its violence and episodic melodrama, it has the seeds of greatness, and modern productions have shown that it can be extremely effective in staging. It makes rewarding reading for all Shakespeare students.

Details of Shakespeare's early life are scanty. He was born the son of a prosperous merchant of Stratford-upon-Avon, and tradition has it that he was born on 23rd April 1564; records show that he was baptized three days later. It is likely that he attended the local grammar school, but he had no university education. Of his early career there is no record, though John Aubrey states that he was, for a time, a country schoolmaster. How he became involved with the stage is equally uncertain, but he was sufficiently established as a playwright by 1592 to be criticised in print. He was a leading member of the Lord Chamberlain's company, which became the King's Men on the accession of James I in 1603. Shakespeare married Anne Hathaway in 1582, by whom he had two daughters and a son, Hamnet, who died in childhood. Towards the end of his life he loosened his ties with London, and retired to New Place, his substantial property in Stratford that he had bought in 1597. He died on 23rd April 1616 aged 52, and is buried in Holy Trinity Church, Stratford.

Further reading:

Themes and Conventions of Elizabethan tragedy,
    M. C. Bradbrook, 1935
Induction to Tragedy, Howard Baker, 1939
Shakespeare's History Plays, E. M. W. Tillyard, 1944

TITUS ANDRONICUS

The scene: Rome, and the country near by

CHARACTERS IN THE PLAY

SATURNINUS, *son to the late Emperor of Rome, afterwards Emperor*

BASSIANUS, *brother to Saturninus*

TITUS ANDRONICUS, *a noble Roman*

MARCUS ANDRONICUS, *tribune of the people, and brother to Titus*

LUCIUS
QUINTUS
MARTIUS
MUTIUS
} *sons to Titus Andronicus*

Young LUCIUS, *a boy, son to Lucius*

PUBLIUS, *son to Marcus Andronicus*

ÆMILIUS, *a noble Roman*

ALARBUS
DEMETRIUS
CHIRON
} *sons to Tamora*

AARON, *a Moor, beloved by Tamora*

A Captain, Tribune, Messenger, and Clown; Romans and Goths

TAMORA, *Queen of the Goths*

LAVINIA, *daughter to Titus Andronicus*

Nurse, and a blackamoor Child

Kinsmen of Titus, Senators, Tribunes, Officers, Soldiers, and Attendants

TITUS ANDRONICUS

[I. I.] *An open place in Rome, before the Capitol, beside the entrance to which there stands the monument of the Andronici. Through a window opening on to the balcony of an upper chamber in the Capitol may be seen the Senate in session. Drums and trumpets are heard*

SATURNINUS and his followers march into the square on one side; BASSIANUS and his followers on the other

Saturninus. Noble patricians, patrons of my right,
Defend the justice of my cause with arms;
And, countrymen, my loving followers.
Plead my successive title with your swords:
I am his first-born son, that was the last
That ware the imperial diadem of Rome;
Then let my father's honours live in me,
Nor wrong mine age with this indignity.
Bassianus. Romans, friends, followers, favourers of
      my right,
If ever Bassianus, Cæsar's son,   10
Were gracious in the eyes of royal Rome,
Keep then this passage to the Capitol,
And suffer not dishonour to approach
The imperial seat, to virtue consecrate,
To justice, continence, and nobility:
But let desert in pure election shine,
And, Romans, fight for freedom in your choice.

*MARCUS ANDRONICUS comes forward on to the balcony
      bearing a crown in his hands*

Marcus. Princes, that strive by factions and by friends
Ambitiously for rule and empery,

20 Know that the people of Rome, for whom we stand
A special party, have by common voice,
In election for the Roman empery,
Chosen Andronicus, surnaméd Pius
For many good and great deserts to Rome.
A nobler man, a braver warrior,
Lives not this day within the city walls.
He by the senate is accited home
From weary wars against the barbarous Goths;
That with his sons, a terror to our foes,
30 Hath yoked a nation strong, trained up in arms.
Ten years are spent since first he undertook
This cause of Rome, and chastiséd with arms
Our enemies' pride: five times he hath returned
Bleeding to Rome, bearing his valiant sons
In coffins from the field [and at this day
To the monument of the Andronici
Done sacrifice of expiation,
And slain the noblest prisoner of the Goths.]
And now at last, laden with honour's spoils,
Returns the good Andronicus to Rome,
Renownéd Titus, flourishing in arms.
Let us entreat, by honour of his name,
Whom worthily you would have now succeed,
And in the Capitol and senate's right,
Whom you pretend to honour and adore,
That you withdraw you and abate your strength,
Dismiss your followers, and, as suitors should,
Plead your deserts in peace and humbleness.
  Saturninus. How fair the tribune speaks to calm
    my thoughts!
  Bassianus. Marcus Andronicus, so I do affy
In thy uprightness and integrity,
And so I love and honour thee and thine,

Thy nobler brother Titus and his sons,   50
And her to whom my thoughts are humbled all,
Gracious Lavinia, Rome's rich ornament,
That I will here dismiss my loving friends;
And to my fortune's and the people's favour
Commit my cause in balance to be weighed.

                              [his followers disperse

Saturninus. Friends, that have been thus forward in
    my right,
I thank you all, and here dismiss you all,
And to the love and favour of my country
Commit myself, my person, and the cause.

                              [his followers disperse

Rome, be as just and gracious unto me,   60
As I am confident and kind to thee.
Open the gates and let me in.

  Bassianus. Tribunes, and me, a poor competitor.

                   [they go up into the Senate-house

Enter a Captain

  Captain. Romans, make way! the good Andronicus,
Patron of virtue, Rome's best champion,
Successful in the battles that he fights,
With honour and with fortune is returned,
From where he circumscribéd with his sword,
And brought to yoke, the enemies of Rome.

A sound of drums and trumpets. Then enter in procession
MUTIUS and MARTIUS, two soldiers bearing a coffin
covered with black, QUINTUS and LUCIUS, and TITUS
ANDRONICUS, followed by his prisoners TAMORA Queen of
the Goths, her sons ALARBUS, CHIRON, and DEMETRIUS,
AARON the Moor, and others. The soldiers set down the
coffin, and TITUS speaks

70 *Titus.* Hail, Rome, victorious in thy mourning weeds!
     Lo, as the bark that hath discharged his fraught
     Returns with precious lading to the bay
     From whence at first she weighed her anchorage,
     Cometh Andronicus, bound with laurel boughs,
     To re-salute his country with his tears,
     Tears of true joy for his return to Rome.
     Thou great defender of this Capitol,
     Stand gracious to the rites that we intend!
     Romans, of five and twenty valiant sons,
80 Half of the number that King Priam had,
     Behold the poor remains, alive and dead!
     These that survive let Rome reward with love;
     These that I bring unto their latest home,
     With burial amongst their ancestors.
     Here Goths have given me leave to sheathe my sword.
     Titus, unkind and careless of thine own,
     Why suffer'st thou thy sons, unburied yet,
     To hover on the dreadful shore of Styx?
     Make way to lay them by their bretheren.

                              [*they open the tomb*

90 There greet in silence, as the dead are wont,
     And sleep in peace, slain in your country's wars!
     O sacred receptacle of my joys,
     Sweet cell of virtue and nobility,
     How many sons hast thou of mine in store,
     That thou wilt never render to me more!
       Lucius. Give us the proudest prisoner of the Goths,
     That we may hew his limbs, and on a pile
     'Ad manes fratrum' sacrifice his flesh,
     Before this earthy prison of their bones,
100 That so the shadows be not unappeased,
     Nor we disturbed with prodigies on earth.
       Titus. I give him you, the noblest that survives,

The eldest son of this distresséd queen.
  Tamora. Stay, Roman brethren! Gracious conqueror,
Victorious Titus, rue the tears I shed,
A mother's tears in passion for her son:
And if thy sons were ever dear to thee,
O, think my son to be as dear to me!
Sufficeth not that we are brought to Rome,
To beautify thy triumphs and return,   110
Captive to thee and to thy Roman yoke;
But must my sons be slaughtered in the streets,
For valiant doings in their country's cause?
O, if to fight for king and commonweal
Were piety in thine, it is in these:
Andronicus, stain not thy tomb with blood.
Wilt thou draw near the nature of the gods?
Draw near them then in being merciful:
Sweet mercy is nobility's true badge;
Thrice-noble Titus, spare my first-born son.   120
  Titus. Patient yourself, madam, and pardon me.
These are their brethren, whom your Goths beheld
Alive and dead, and for their brethren slain
Religiously they ask a sacrifice:
To this your son is marked, and die he must,
T' appease their groaning shadows that are gone.
  Lucius. Away with him! and make a fire straight,
And with our swords, upon a pile of wood,
Let's hew his limbs till they be clean consumed.
              [*the sons of Titus hale Alarbus forth*
  Tamora. O cruel, irreligious piety!   130
  Chiron. Was never Scythia half so barbarous.
  Demetrius. Oppose not Scythia to ambitious Rome.
Alarbus goes to rest, and we survive
To tremble under Titus' threat'ning look.
Then, madam, stand resolved, but hope withal

The self-same gods that armed the Queen of Troy
With opportunity of sharp revenge
Upon the Thracian tyrant in her tent
May favour Tamora, the Queen of Goths,
140 (When Goths were Goths and Tamora was queen)
To quit the bloody wrongs upon her foes.

> *Enter the sons of Andronicus again,*
> *with their swords bloody*

Lucius. See, lord and father, how we have performed
Our Roman rites! Alarbus' limbs are lopped,
And entrails feed the sacrificing fire,
Whose smoke like incense doth perfume the sky.
Remaineth naught but to inter our brethren,
And with loud 'larums welcome them to Rome.
Titus. Let it be so, and let Andronicus
Make this his latest farewell to their souls.

> *[trumpets sounded and the coffin laid in the tomb*

150 In peace and honour rest you here, my sons,
Rome's readiest champions, repose you here in rest,
Secure from worldly chances and mishaps!
Here lurks no treason, here no envy swells,
Here grow no damnéd drugs, here are no storms,
No noise, but silence and eternal sleep:

> *Enter LAVINIA*

In peace and honour rest you here, my sons!
Lavinia. In peace and honour live Lord Titus long,
My noble lord and father, live in fame!
Lo, at this tomb my tributary tears
160 I render for my brethren's obsequies,
And at thy feet I kneel, with tears of joy
Shed on this earth for thy return to Rome.
O, bless me here with thy victorious hand,

Whose fortunes Rome's best citizens applaud.
Titus. Kind Rome, that hast thus lovingly reserved
The cordial of mine age to glad my heart!
Lavinia, live, outlive thy father's days,
And fame's eternal date, for virtue's praise!

Enter above MARCUS ANDRONICUS, SATURNINUS,
BASSIANUS, *and others*

Marcus. Long live Lord Titus, my belovéd brother,
Gracious triumpher in the eyes of Rome!   170
Titus. Thanks, gentle tribune, noble brother Marcus.
Marcus. And welcome, nephews, from
        successful wars,
You that survive, and you that sleep in fame!
Fair lords, your fortunes are alike in all,
That in your country's service drew your swords,
But safer triumph is this funeral pomp,
That hath aspired to Solon's happiness,
And triumphs over chance in honour's bed.
Titus Andronicus, the people of Rome,
Whose friend in justice thou hast ever been,   180
Send thee by me, their tribune and their trust,
This palliament of white and spotless hue,
And name thee in election for the empire
With these our late-deceaséd emperor's sons:
Be 'candidatus' then, and put it on,
And help to set a head on headless Rome.
Titus. A better head her glorious body fits
Than his that shakes for age and feebleness:
What should I don this robe and trouble you?
Be chosen with proclamations to-day,   190
To-morrow yield up rule, resign my life,
And set abroad new business for you all?

Rome, I have been thy soldier forty years,
And led my country's strength successfully,
And buried one and twenty valiant sons,
Knighted in field, slain manfully in arms,
In right and service of their noble country:
Give me a staff of honour for mine age,
But not a sceptre to control the world.
200 Upright he held it, lords, that held it last.
 Marcus. Titus, thou shalt obtain and ask the empery.
 Saturninus. Proud and ambitious tribune, canst
  thou tell?
 Titus. Patience, Prince Saturninus.
 Saturninus.   Romans, do me right.
Patricians, draw your swords and sheathe them not
Till Saturninus be Rome's emperor:
Andronicus, would thou were shipped to hell,
Rather than rob me of the people's hearts.
 Lucius. Proud Saturnine, interrupter of the good
That noble-minded Titus means to thee!
210 *Titus.* Content thee, prince, I will restore to thee
The people's hearts, and wean them from themselves.
 Bassianus. Andronicus, I do not flatter thee,
But honour thee, and will do till I die;
My faction if thou strengthen with thy friends,
I will most thankful be, and thanks to men
Of noble minds is honourable meed.
 Titus. People of Rome, and people's tribunes here,
I ask your voices and your suffrages.
Will ye bestow them friendly on Andronicus?
220 *Tribune.* To gratify the good Andronicus,
And gratulate his safe return to Rome,
The people will accept whom he admits.
 Titus. Tribunes, I thank you, and this suit I make,
That you create our emperor's eldest son,

Lord Saturnine; whose virtues will I hope
Reflect on Rome as Titan's rays on earth,
And ripen justice in this commonweal:
Then if you will elect by my advice,
Crown him, and say, 'Long live our emperor!'

Marcus. With voices and applause of every sort,   230
Patricians and plebeians, we create
Lord Saturninus Rome's great emperor,
And say 'Long live our Emperor Saturnine!'

[*a long flourish till they come down*

Saturninus. Titus Andronicus, for thy favours done
To us in our election this day,
I give thee thanks in part of thy deserts,
And will with deeds requite thy gentleness:
And for an onset, Titus, to advance
Thy name and honourable family,
Lavinia will I make my emperess,   240
Rome's royal mistress, mistress of my heart,
And in the sacred Pantheon her espouse:
Tell me, Andronicus, doth this motion please thee?

Titus. It doth, my worthy lord, and in this match
I hold me highly honoured of your grace,
And here in sight of Rome to Saturnine,
King and commander of our commonweal,
The wide world's emperor, do I consecrate
My sword, my chariot, and my prisoners,
Presents well worthy Rome's imperious lord: 250
Receive them then, the tribute that I owe,
Mine honour's ensigns humbled at thy feet.

Saturninus. Thanks, noble Titus, father of my life!
How proud I am of thee and of thy gifts
Rome shall record, and when I do forget
The least of these unspeakable deserts,
Romans, forget your fealty to me.

Titus [*to Tamora*]. Now, madam, are you prisoner to
　　an emperor,
To him that, for your honour and your state,
260 Will use you nobly and your followers.
　　(*Saturninus*. A goodly lady, trust me! Of the hue
That I would choose, were I to choose anew.
[*aloud*] Clear up, fair queen, that cloudy countenance.
Though chance of war hath wrought this change
　　of cheer,
Thou com'st not to be made a scorn in Rome.
Princely shall be thy usage every way.
Rest on my word, and let not discontent
Daunt all your hopes. Madam, he comforts you
Can make you greater than the Queen of Goths.
270 Lavinia, you are not displeased with this?
　　Lavinia. Not I, my lord, sith true nobility
Warrants these words in princely courtesy.
　　Saturninus. Thanks, sweet Lavinia. Romans,
　　　let us go.
Ransomless here we set our prisoners free.
Proclaim our honours, lords, with trump and drum.
　　　[*Flourish. Saturninus courts Tamora in dumb show*
　　Bassianus [*seizing Lavinia*]. Lord Titus, by your leave,
　　　this maid is mine.
　　Titus. How, sir! are you in earnest then, my lord?
　　Bassianus. Ay, noble Titus, and resolved withal
To do myself this reason and this right.
280 *Marcus*. 'Suum cuique' is our Roman justice.
This prince in justice seizeth but his own.
　　Lucius. And that he will, and shall, if Lucius live.
　　Titus. Traitors, avaunt! Where is the
　　　emperor's guard?
Treason, my lord! Lavinia is surprised!
　　Saturninus. Surprised! by whom?

Bassianus.   By him that justly may
Bear his betrothed from all the world away.
Mutius. Brothers, help to convey her hence away,
And with my sword I'll keep this door safe.

MARCUS, BASSIANUS *and the brothers* LUCIUS, QUINTUS
and MARTIUS *form a bodyguard for* LAVINIA, *as they
leave the square*

Titus. Follow, my lord, and I'll soon bring her back.

SATURNINUS *beckons* TAMORA *aside and they go up
into the Capitol with* AARON *and her sons*

Mutius. My lord, you pass not here.   290
Titus.   What, villain boy!
Barr'st me my way in Rome?   [*they fight*
Mutius [*falling*].   Help, Lucius, help!

LUCIUS *returns*

Lucius. My lord, you are unjust; and more than so,
In wrongful quarrel you have slain your son.
Titus. Nor thou, nor he, are any sons of mine:
My sons would never so dishonour me.
Traitor, restore Lavinia to the emperor.
Lucius. Dead if you will, but not to be his wife,
That is another's lawful promised love.   [*he goes*

*Enter aloft the Emperor with Tamora and her
two sons and Aaron the Moor*

Saturninus. No, Titus, no, the emperor needs her not,
Not her, nor thee, nor any of thy stock: 300
I'll trust by leisure him that mocks me once,
Thee never, nor thy traitorous haughty sons,
Confederates all thus to dishonour me.

Was none in Rome to make a stale
But Saturnine? Full well, Andronicus,
Agree these deeds with that proud brag of thine,
That saidst, I begged the empire at thy hands.
  Titus. O monstrous! what reproachful words are these?
  Saturninus. But go thy ways, go, give that
    changing piece
310 To him that flourished for her with his sword:
A valiant son-in-law thou shalt enjoy,
One fit to bandy with thy lawless sons,
To ruffle in the commonwealth of Rome.
  Titus. These words are razors to my wounded heart.
  Saturninus. And therefore, lovely Tamora, Queen
    of Goths,
That like the stately Phœbe 'mongst her nymphs
Dost overshine the gallant'st dames of Rome,
If thou be pleased with this my sudden choice,
Behold, I choose thee, Tamora, for my bride,
320 And will create thee emperess of Rome.
Speak, Queen of Goths, dost thou applaud my choice?
And here I swear by all the Roman Gods,
Sith priest and holy water are so near,
And tapers burn so bright, and every thing
In readiness for Hymenæus stand,
I will not re-salute the streets of Rome,
Or climb my palace, till from forth this place
I lead espoused my bride along with me.
  Tamora. And here in sight of heaven to Rome I swear,
330 If Saturnine advance the Queen of Goths,
She will a handmaid be to his desires,
A loving nurse, a mother to his youth.
  Saturninus. Ascend, fair queen, Pantheon.
    Lords, accompany
Your noble emperor and his lovely bride,

Sent by the heavens for Prince Saturnine,
Whose wisdom hath her fortune conqueréd.
There shall we consummate our spousal rites.

[they go within

  Titus. I am not bid to wait upon this bride.
Titus, when wert thou wont to walk alone,
Dishonoured thus and challengéd of wrongs?   340

Re-enter MARCUS, LUCIUS, QUINTUS, *and* MARTIUS

  Marcus. O Titus, see, O, see, what thou hast done!
In a bad quarrel slain a virtuous son.
  Titus. No, foolish tribune, no; no son of mine,
Nor thou, nor these, confederates in the deed
That hath dishonoured all our family,
Unworthy brother, and unworthy sons!
  Lucius. But let us give him burial as becomes;
Give Mutius burial with our bretheren.
  Titus. Traitors, away! he rests not in this tomb:
This monument five hundred years hath stood,   350
Which I have sumptuously re-edified:
Here none but soldiers and Rome's servitors
Repose in fame; none basely slain in brawls.
Bury him where you can, he comes not here.
  Marcus. My lord, this is impiety in you.
My nephew Mutius' deeds do plead for him,
He must be buried with his bretheren.
  Quintus, Martius. And shall, or him we will
    accompany.
  Titus. And shall? what villain was it spake that word?
  Quintus. He that would vouch it in any place but here. 360
  Titus. What, would you bury him in my despite?
  Marcus. No, noble Titus, but entreat of thee
To pardon Mutius and to bury him.

Titus. Marcus, even thou hast struck upon my crest,
And with these boys mine honour thou hast wounded.
My foes I do repute you every one,
So trouble me no more, but get you gone.
Martius. He is not with himself, let us withdraw.
Quintus. Not I, till Mutius' bones be buried.

> [*the brother and the sons kneel*

370 *Marcus.* Brother, for in that name doth nature plead,—
Quintus. Father, and in that name doth
            nature speak,—
Titus. Speak thou no more, if all the rest will speed.
Marcus. Renownéd Titus, more than half my soul
Lucius. Dear father, soul and substance of us all—
Marcus. Suffer thy brother Marcus to inter
His noble nephew here in virtue's nest,
That died in honour and Lavinia's cause.
Thou art a Roman, be not barbarous:
The Greeks upon advice did bury Ajax
380 That slew himself; and wise Laertes' son
Did graciously plead for his funerals:
Let not young Mutius then, that was thy joy,
Be barred his entrance here.
Titus.   Rise, Marcus, rise.
The dismal'st day is this that e'er I saw,
To be dishonoured by my sons in Rome!
Well, bury him, and bury me the next.

They put him in the tomb

Lucius. There lie thy bones, sweet Mutius, with
      thy friends,
Till we with trophies do adorn thy tomb.

They all kneel and say

All. No man shed tears for noble Mutius,
390 He lives in fame that died in virtue's cause.

Marcus. My lord, to step out of these dreary dumps,
How comes it that the subtle Queen of Goths
Is of a sudden thus advanced in Rome?
Titus. I know not, Marcus, but I know it is,
(Whether by device or no, the heavens can tell.)
Is she not then beholding to the man
That brought her for this high good turn so far?
Yes, and will nobly him remunerate.

*Re-enter, from one side, SATURNINUS attended, TAMORA,
DEMETRIUS, CHIRON, and AARON; from the other,
BASSIANUS, LAVINIA, with others*

Saturninus. So Bassianus, you have played your prize:
God give you joy, sir, of your gallant bride!   400
Bassianus. And you of yours, my lord! I say no more,
Nor wish no less, and so I take my leave.
Saturninus. Traitor, if Rome have law, or we
    have power,
Thou and thy faction shall repent this rape.
Bassianus. Rape, call you it, my lord, to seize my own,
My true-betrothéd love, and now my wife?
But let the laws of Rome determine all,
Meanwhile am I possessed of that is mine.
Saturninus. 'Tis good, sir; you are very short with us,
But if we live we'll be as sharp with you.   410
Bassianus. My lord, what I have done, as best I may
Answer I must, and shall do with my life.
Only thus much I give your grace to know—
By all the duties that I owe to Rome,
This noble gentleman, Lord Titus here,
Is in opinion and in honour wronged;
That in the rescue of Lavinia
With his own hand did slay his youngest son,
In zeal to you and highly moved to wrath

420 To be controlled in that he frankly gave.
Receive him then to favour, Saturnine,
That hath expressed himself in all his deeds
A father and a friend to thee and Rome.
  Titus. Prince Bassianus, leave to plead my deeds,
'Tis thou and those that have dishonoured me.
Rome and the righteous heavens be my judge,
How I have loved and honoured Saturnine!
  Tamora. My worthy lord, if ever Tamora
Were gracious in those princely eyes of thine,
430 Then hear me speak indifferently for all;
And at my suit, sweet, pardon what is past.
  Saturninus. What, madam! be dishonoured openly,
And basely put it up without revenge?
  Tamora. Not so, my lord, the gods of Rome forfend
I should be author to dishonour you!
But on mine honour dare I undertake
For good Lord Titus' innocence in all,
Whose fury not dissembled speaks his griefs:
Then at my suit look graciously on him,
440 Lose not so noble a friend on vain suppose,
Nor with sour looks afflict his gentle heart.
[*Aside*] My lord, be ruled by me, be won at last,
Dissemble all your griefs and discontents—
You are but newly planted in your throne—
Lest then the people, and patricians too,
Upon a just survey, take Titus' part,
And so supplant you for ingratitude,
Which Rome reputes to be a heinous sin.
Yield at entreats: and then let me alone,
450 I'll find a day to massacre them all,
And raze their faction and their family,
The cruel father and his traitorous sons,
To whom I suéd for my dear son's life;

And make them know what 'tis to let a queen
Kneel in the streets and beg for grace in vain.
[*Aloud*] Come, come, sweet emperor—
    come, Andronicus—
Take up this good old man, and cheer the heart
That dies in tempest of thy angry frown.
  Saturninus. Rise, Titus, rise, my empress
    hath prevailed.
  Titus. I thank your majesty, and her, my lord.   460
These words, these looks, infuse new life in me.
  Tamora. Titus, I am incorporate in Rome,
A Roman now adopted happily,
And must advise the emperor for his good.
This day all quarrels die, Andronicus.
And let it be mine honour, good my lord,
That I have reconciled your friends and you.
For you, Prince Bassianus, I have passed
My word and promise to the emperor,
That you will be more mild and tractable.   470
And fear not, lords, and you, Lavinia;
By my advice, all humbled on your knees, [*they kneel*
You shall ask pardon of his majesty.
  Lucius. We do, and vow to heaven, and to his highness,
That what we did was mildly as we might,
Tend'ring our sister's honour and our own.
  Marcus. That on mine honour here do I protest.
  Saturninus. Away, and talk not, trouble us no more.
  Tamora. Nay, nay, sweet emperor, we must all
    be friends.
The tribune and his nephews kneel for grace.   480
I will not be denied. Sweet heart, look back.
  Saturninus. Marcus, for thy sake, and thy
    brother's here,
And at my lovely Tamora's entreats,

I do remit these young men's heinous faults.
Stand up.
Lavinia, though you left me like a churl,
I found a friend, and sure as death I swore
I would not part a bachelor from the priest.
Come, if the emperor's court can feast two brides,
490 You are my guest, Lavinia, and your friends.
This day shall be a love-day, Tamora.
    Titus. To-morrow, an it please your majesty
To hunt the panther and the hart with me,
With horn and hound we'll give your grace bonjour.
    Saturninus. Be it so, Titus, and gramercy too.

      They troop out with trumpets blowing.
           Aaron remains

[2. 1.] *Aaron.* Now climbeth Tamora Olympus' top,
Safe out of fortune's shot, and sits aloft,
Secure of thunder's crack or lightning flash,
Advanced above pale envy's threat'ning reach.
As when the golden sun salutes the morn,
And having gilt the ocean with his beams,
Gallops the zodiac in his glistering coach,
And overlooks the highest-peering hills;
So Tamora.
10 Upon her wit doth earthly honour wait,
And virtue stoops and trembles at her frown.
Then, Aaron, arm thy heart, and fit thy thoughts,
To mount aloft with thy imperial mistress,
And mount her pitch, whom thou in triumph long
Hast prisoner held, fettered in amorous chains,
And faster bound to Aaron's charming eyes,
Than is Prometheus tied to Caucasus.
Away with slavish weeds and servile thoughts!
I will be bright, and shine in pearl and gold,

To wait upon this new-made emperess.   20
To wait, said I? to wanton with this queen,
This goddess, this Semiramis, this nymph,
This siren, that will charm Rome's Saturnine,
And see his shipwreck and his commonweal's.
Holloa! what storm is this?   [*he steps aside*

Enter CHIRON and DEMETRIUS, *braving*

Demetrius. Chiron, thy years want wit, thy wits
    want edge,
And manners, to intrude where I am graced,
And may for aught thou know'st affected be.
 Chiron. Demetrius, thou dost overween in all,
And so in this, to bear me down with braves.   30
'Tis not the difference of a year or two
Makes me less gracious, or thee more fortunate;
I am as able and as fit as thou
To serve, and to deserve my mistress' grace,
And that my sword upon thee shall approve,
And plead my passions for Lavinia's love.
 (*Aaron.* Clubs, clubs! these lovers will not keep
    the peace.
 Demetrius. Why, boy, although our
    mother, unadvised,
Gave you a dancing-rapier by your side,
Are you so desperate grown, to threat your friends?   40
Go to; have your lath glued within your sheath,
Till you know better how to handle it.
 Chiron. Meanwhile, sir, with the little skill I have,
Full well shalt thou perceive how much I dare.
 Demetrius. Ay, boy, grow ye so brave?   [*they draw*
 Aaron [*comes forward*].   Why, how now, lords
So near the emperor's palace dare ye draw,
And maintain such a quarrel openly?

Full well I wot the ground of all this grudge.
I would not for a million of gold
50 The cause were known to them it most concerns,
Nor would your noble mother for much more
Be so dishonoured in the court of Rome.
For shame, put up.

    Demetrius.   Not I, till I have sheathed
My rapier in his bosom, and withal
Thrust those reproachful speeches down his throat,
That he hath breathed in my dishonour here.

    Chiron. For that I am prepared and full resolved,
Foul-spoken coward, that thund'rest with thy tongue
And with thy weapon nothing dar'st perform.

60   *Aaron.* Away, I say!
Now, by the gods that warlike Goths adore,
This petty brabble will undo us all.
Why, lords, and think you not how dangerous
It is to jet upon a prince's right?
What, is Lavinia then become so loose,
Or Bassianus so degenerate,
That for her love such quarrels may be broached
Without controlment, justice, or revenge?
Young lords, beware! an should the empress know
70 This discord's ground, the music would not please.

    Chiron. I care not, I, knew she and all the world:
I love Lavinia more than all the world.

    Demetrius. Youngling, learn thou to make some
         meaner choice.
Lavinia is thine elder brother's hope.

    Aaron. Why, are ye mad? or know ye not, in Rome
How furious and impatient they be,
And cannot brook competitors in love?
I tell you, lords, you do but plot your deaths
By this device.

Chiron.   Aaron, a thousand deaths
Would I propose to achieve her whom I love.   80
    Aaron. To achieve her how?
    Demetrius.   Why mak'st thou it so strange?
She is a woman, therefore may be wooed;
She is a woman, therefore may be won;
She is Lavinia, therefore must be loved.
What, man! more water glideth by the mill
Than wots the miller of, and easy it is
Of a cut loaf to steal a shive, we know:
Though Bassianus be the emperor's brother,
Better than he have worn Vulcan's badge.
    (*Aaron.* Ay, and as good as Saturninus may.   90
    Demetrius. Then why should he despair that knows
          to court it
With words, fair looks, and liberality?
What, hast thou not full often struck a doe,
And borne her cleanly by the keeper's nose?
    Aaron. Why then, it seems, some certain snatch or so
Would serve your turns.
    Chiron.   Ay, so the turn were served.
    Demetrius. Aaron, thou hast hit it.
    Aaron.   Would you had hit it too,
Then should not we be tired with this ado.
Why, hark ye, hark ye! and are you such fools
To square for this? would it offend you then   100
That both should speed?
    Chiron.   Faith, not me.
    Demetrius. Nor me, so I were one.
    Aaron. For shame, be friends, and join for that you jar.
'Tis policy and stratagem must do
That you affect, and so must you resolve,
That what you cannot as you would achieve,
You must perforce accomplish as you may.

Take this of me, Lucrece was not more chaste
Than this Lavinia, Bassianus' love.
110 A speedier course than ling'ring languishment
Must we pursue, and I have found the path.
My lords, a solemn hunting is in hand,
There will the lovely Roman ladies troop:
The forest walks are wide and spacious,
And many unfrequented plots there are
Fitted by kind for rape and villainy:
Single you thither then this dainty doe,
And strike her home by force, if not by words:
This way, or not at all, stand you in hope.
120 Come, come, our empress, with her sacred wit
To villainy and vengeance consecrate,
Will we acquaint with all that we intend,
And she shall file our engines with advice,
That will not suffer you to square yourselves,
But to your wishes' height advance you both.
The emperor's court is like the House of Fame,
The palace full of tongues, of eyes, and ears:
The woods are ruthless, dreadful, deaf, and dull;
There speak, and strike, brave boys, and take your turns,
130 There serve your lust shadowed from heaven's eye,
And revel in Lavinia's treasury.
    Chiron. Thy counsel, lad, smells of no cowardice.
    Demetrius. 'Sit fas aut nefas', till I find the stream
To cool this heat, a charm to calm these fits,
'Per Styga, per manes vehor'.   [*they go*

[2. 2.]   *A glade in a forest near Rome*

*Enter TITUS ANDRONICUS with his three sons and
MARCUS, making a noise with hounds and horns*

Titus. The hunt is up, the morn is bright and grey,
The fields are fragrant, and the woods are green:
Uncouple here, and let us make a bay,
And wake the emperor and his lovely bride,
And rouse the prince, and ring a hunter's peal,
That all the court may echo with the noise.
Sons, let it be your charge, as it is ours,
To attend the emperor's person carefully:
I have been troubled in my sleep this night,
But dawning day new comfort hath inspired.   10

*Here a cry of hounds, and wind horns in a peal: then
enter SATURNINUS, TAMORA, BASSIANUS, LAVINIA,
CHIRON, DEMETRIUS, and their attendants*

Many good morrows to your majesty!
Madam, to you as many and as good!
I promiséd your grace a hunter's peal.
   Saturninus. And you have rung it lustily, my lords,
Somewhat too early for new-married ladies.
   Bassianus. Lavinia, how say you?
   Lavinia.   I say, no;
I have been broad awake two hours and more.
   Saturninus. Come on then, horse and chariots let
      us have,
And to our sport. [*To Tamora*] Madam, now shall
      ye see
Our Roman hunting.
   Marcus.   I have dogs, my lord,   20
Will rouse the proudest panther in the chase,
And climb the highest promontory top.

Titus. And I have horse will follow where the game
Makes way and run like swallows o'er the plain.
Demetrius. Chiron, we hunt not, we, with horse
  nor hound,
But hope to pluck a dainty doe to ground.   [*they go*

[2. 3.]   *Enter AARON alone, with a bag of gold*

Aaron. He that had wit would think that I had none,
To bury so much gold under a tree,
And never after to inherit it.
Let him that thinks of me so abjectly
Know that this gold must coin a stratagem,
Which, cunningly effected, will beget
A very excellent piece of villainy:
And so repose, sweet gold, for their unrest,
That have their alms out of the empress' chest.

                          [*hides the gold*

Enter TAMORA alone to the Moor

10 *Tamora.* My lovely Aaron, wherefore look'st thou sad,
When every thing doth make a gleeful boast?
The birds chaunt melody on every bush,
The snake lies rolléd in the cheerful sun,
The green leaves quiver with the cooling wind,
And make a chequered shadow on the ground:
Under their sweet shade, Aaron, let us sit,
And whilst the babbling echo mocks the hounds,
Replying shrilly to the well-tuned horns,
As if a double hunt were heard at once,
20 Let us sit down and mark their yellowing noise:
And after conflict such as was supposed
The wandering prince and Dido once enjoyed,
When with a happy storm they were surprised,
And curtained with a counsel-keeping cave,

We may, each wreathéd in the other's arms,
(Our pastimes done) possess a golden slumber,
Whiles hounds and horns and sweet melodious birds
Be unto us as is a nurse's song
Of lullaby to bring her babe asleep.

 Aaron. Madam, though Venus govern your desires, 30
Saturn is dominator over mine:
What signifies my deadly-standing eye,
My silence and my cloudy melancholy,
My fleece of woolly hair that now uncurls
Even as an adder when she doth unroll
To do some fatal execution?
No, madam, these are no venereal signs:
Vengeance is in my heart, death in my hand,
Blood and revenge are hammering in my head.
Hark, Tamora, the empress of my soul, 40
Which never hopes more heaven than rests in thee,
This is the day of doom for Bassianus:
His Philomel must lose her tongue to-day,
Thy sons make pillage of her chastity,
And wash their hands in Bassianus' blood.
Seest thou this letter? take it up, I pray thee,
And give the king this fatal-plotted scroll.
Now question me no more; we are espied;
Here comes a parcel of our hopeful booty,
Which dreads not yet their lives' destruction. 50

Enter BASSIANUS and LAVINIA

 Tamora. Ah, my sweet Moor, sweeter to me than life!
 Aaron. No more, great empress, Bassianus comes.
Be cross with him, and I'll go fetch thy sons
To back thy quarrels whatsoe'er they be. *[he goes*
 Bassianus. Who have we here? Rome's
  royal emperess,

Unfurnished of her well-beseeming troop?
Or is it Dian, habited like her,
Who hath abandonéd her holy groves
To see the general hunting in this forest?

60 *Tamora.* Saucy controller of my private steps!
Had I the power that some say Dian had,
Thy temples should be planted presently
With horns, as was Actæon's, and the hounds
Should drive upon thy new-transforméd limbs,
Unmannerly intruder as thou art!

Lavinia. Under your patience, gentle emperess,
'Tis thought you have a goodly gift in horning,
And to be doubted that your Moor and you
Are singled forth to try experiments:

70 Jove shield your husband from his hounds to-day!
'Tis pity they should take him for a stag.

Bassianus. Believe me, queen, your
    swarth Cimmerian
Doth make your honour of his body's hue,
Spotted, detested, and abominable.
Why are you séquest'réd from all your train,
Dismounted from your snow-white goodly steed,
And wandered hither to an obscure plot,
Accompanied but with a barbarous Moor,
If foul desire had not conducted you?

80 *Lavinia.* And, being intercepted in your sport,
Great reason that my noble lord be rated
For sauciness. I pray you, let us hence,
And let her joy her raven-coloured love,
This valley fits the purpose passing well.

Bassianus. The king my brother shall have note
    of this.

Lavinia. Ay, for these slips have made him
    noted long.

Good king, to be so mightily abused!
  Tamora. Why have I patience to endure all this?

      Enter CHIRON and DEMETRIUS

  Demetrius. How now, dear sovereign, and our
    gracious mother,
Why doth your highness look so pale and wan?   90
  Tamora. Have I not reason, think you, to look pale?
These two have ticed me hither to this place,
A barren detested vale, you see it is;
The trees, though summer, yet forlorn and lean,
O'ercome with moss and baleful mistletoe:
Here never shines the sun; here nothing breeds,
Unless the nightly owl or fatal raven:
And when they showed me this abhorréd pit,
They told me, here, at dead time of the night
A thousand fiends, a thousand hissing snakes,   100
Ten thousand swelling toads, as many urchins,
Would make such fearful and confuséd cries,
As any mortal body hearing it
Should straight fall mad, or else die suddenly.
No sooner had they told this hellish tale,
But straight they told me they would bind me here
Unto the body of a dismal yew,
And leave me to this miserable death.
And then they called me foul adulteress,
Lascivious Goth, and all the bitterest terms   110
That ever ear did hear to such effect.
And, had you not by wondrous fortune come,
This vengeance on me had they executed:
Revenge it, as you love your mother's life,
Or be ye not henceforth my children called.
  Demetrius. This is a witness that I am thy son.
                        [stabs Bassianus

Chiron. And this for me, struck home to show
　　my strength.　　　　　　　*[stabbing him likewise*
Lavinia. Ay come, Semiramis, nay,
　　barbarous Tamora!
For no name fits thy nature but thy own!
120 *Tamora.* Give me the poniard! you shall know,
　　my boys,
Your mother's hand shall right your mother's wrong.
Demetrius. Stay, madam, here is more belongs to her.
First thrash the corn, then after burn the straw:
This minion stood upon her chastity,
Upon her nuptial vow, her loyalty,
And with that painted hope she braves your mightiness:
And shall she carry this unto her grave?
Chiron. An if she do, I would I were an eunuch.
Drag hence her husband to some secret hole,
130 And make his dead trunk pillow to our lust.
Tamora. But when ye have the honey ye desire,
Let not this wasp outlive, us both to sting.
Chiron. I warrant you, madam, we will make
　　that sure:
Come, mistress, now perforce we will enjoy
That nice-preservéd honesty of yours.
Lavinia. O Tamora! thou bear'st a woman's face—
Tamora. I will not hear her speak, away with her.
Lavinia. Sweet lords, entreat her hear me but a word.
Demetrius. Listen, fair madam, let it be your glory
140 To see her tears, but be your heart to them
As unrelenting flint to drops of rain.
Lavinia. When did the tiger's young ones teach
　　the dam?
O, do not learn her wrath; she taught it thee.
The milk thou suck'dst from her did turn to marble,
Even at thy teat thou hadst thy tyranny.

Yet every mother breeds not sons alike,

[to Chiron

Do thou entreat her show a woman's pity.

　Chiron. What! wouldst thou have me prove myself
　　a bastard?

　Lavinia. 'Tis true; the raven doth not hatch a lark:
Yet I have heard—O could I find it now!—　　　　150
The lion, moved with pity, did endure
To have his princely paws pared all away:
Some say that ravens foster forlorn children,
The whilst their own birds famish in their nests:
O, be to me, though thy hard heart say no,
Nothing so kind but something pitiful!

　Tamora. I know not what it means, away with her!

　Lavinia. O, let me teach thee for my father's sake,
That gave thee life when well he might have slain thee.
Be not obdurate, open thy deaf ears.　　　　160

　Tamora. Hadst thou in person ne'er offended me,
Even for his sake am I pitiless.
Remember, boys, I poured forth tears in vain
To save your brother from the sacrifice,
But fierce Andronicus would not relent.
Therefore away with her, and use her as you will;
The worse to her, the better loved of me.

　Lavinia [*clasps her knees*]. O Tamora, be called
　　a gentle queen,
And with thine own hands kill me in this place!
For 'tis not life that I have begged so long,　　　170
Poor I was slain when Bassianus died.

　Tamora. What begg'st thou then? fond woman, let
　　me go.

　Lavinia. 'Tis present death I beg, and one thing more
That womanhood denies my tongue to tell.
O, keep me from their worse than killing lust,

And tumble me into some loathsome pit,
Where never man's eye may behold my body
Do this, and be a charitable murderer.
    Tamora. So should I rob my sweet sons of their fee.
180 No, let them satisfy their lust on thee.
    Demetrius. Away! for thou hast staid us here too long.
    Lavinia. No grace? no womanhood? Ah
        beastly creature!
The blot and enemy to our general name!
Confusion fall——
    Chiron. Nay, then I'll stop your mouth [*he gags her*].
                      Bring thou her husband.
This is the hole where Aaron bid us hide him.

*Demetrius heaves the corpse into a pit, thereafter covering
it with branches; the two then go off dragging Lavinia
between them*

    Tamora. Farewell, my sons, see that you make
        her sure.
Ne'er let my heart know merry cheer indeed
Till all the Andronici be made away.
190 Now will I hence to seek my lovely Moor,
And let my spleenful sons this trull deflower. [*she goes*

*Enter from another direction, AARON
with QUINTUS and MARTIUS*

    Aaron. Come on, my lords, the better foot before!
Straight will I bring you to the loathsome pit
Where I espied the panther fast asleep.
    Quintus. My sight is very dull, whate'er it bodes.
    Martius. And mine, I promise you: were it not
        for shame,
Well could I leave our sport to sleep awhile.
                      [*he falls into the pit*

Quintus. What, art thou fallen? What subtle hole
    is this,
Whose mouth is covered with rude-growing briers,
Upon whose leaves are drops of new-shed blood   200
As fresh as morning dew distilled on flowers?
A very fatal place it seems to me.
Speak, brother, hast thou hurt thee with the fall?
  Martius. O, brother, with the dismall'st object hurt
That ever eye with sight made heart lament.
  (*Aaron.* Now will I fetch the king to find them here,
That he thereby may have a likely guess,
How these were they that made away his brother.
                                   [*he goes*
  Martius. Why dost not comfort me, and help me out
From this unhallowed and blood-stainéd hole?   210
  Quintus. I am surpriséd with an uncouth fear,
A chilling sweat o'er-runs my trembling joints,
My heart suspects more than mine eye can see.
  Martius. To prove thou hast a true-divining heart,
Aaron and thou look down into this den,
And see a fearful sight of blood and death.
  Quintus. Aaron is gone, and my compassionate heart
Will not permit mine eyes once to behold
The thing whereat it trembles by surmise:
O, tell me who it is, for ne'er till now   220
Was I a child to fear I know not what.
  Martius.† Lord Bassianus lies berayed in blood,
All on a heap, like to a slaughtered lamb,
In this detested, dark, blood-drinking pit.
  Quintus. If it be dark, how dost thou know 'tis he?
  Martius. Upon his bloody finger he doth wear
A precious ring, that lightens all this hole,
Which, like a taper in some monument,
Doth shine upon the dead man's earthy cheeks,

230 And shows the ragged entrails of this pit:
So pale did shine the moon on Pyramus,
When he by night lay bathed in maiden blood.
O brother, help me with thy fainting hand—
If fear hath made thee faint, as me it hath—
Out of this fell devouring receptacle,
As hateful as Cocytus' misty mouth.
    Quintus. Reach me thy hand, that I may help thee out;
Or, wanting strength to do thee so much good,
I may be plucked into the swallowing womb
240 Of this deep pit, poor Bassianus' grave.   [*he strives*
I have no strength to pluck thee to the brink.
    Martius. Nor I no strength to climb without thy help.
    Quintus. Thy hand once more, I will not loose again,
Till thou art here aloft or I below: [*he strives again*
Thou canst not come to me, I come to thee.
                        [*he falls in*

        Enter the Emperor and AARON *the Moor*

    Saturninus. Along with me! I'll see what hole is here,
And what he is that now is leaped into it.
Say, who art thou, that lately didst descend
Into this gaping hollow of the earth?
250   *Martius.* The unhappy sons of old Andronicus,
Brought hither in a most unlucky hour,
To find thy brother Bassianus dead.
    Saturninus. My brother dead! I know thou dost
        but jest:
He and his lady both are at the lodge,
Upon the north side of this pleasant chase;
'Tis not an hour since I left them there.
    Martius. We know not where you left them all alive,
But, out alas! here have we found him dead.

Enter TAMORA, ANDRONICUS, *and* LUCIUS

Tamora. Where is my lord the king?

Saturninus. Here, Tamora, though grieved with
    killing grief.   260

Tamora. Where is thy brother, Bassianus?

Saturninus. Now to the bottom dost thou search
    my wound;

Poor Bassianus here lies muderéd.

  Tamora. Then all too late I bring this fatal writ,

The complot of this timeless tragedy;

And wonder greatly that man's face can fold

In pleasing smiles such murderous tyranny.

                            [she giveth Saturnine a letter

Saturninus [*reads*]. 'An if we miss to meet
    him handsomely—

Sweet huntsman, Bassianus 'tis we mean—

Do thou so much as dig the grave for him.   270

Thou know'st our meaning. Look for thy reward

Among the nettles at the elder tree,

Which overshades the mouth of that same pit

Where we decreed to bury Bassianus.

Do this and purchase us thy lasting friends.'

O, Tamora! was ever heard the like?

This is the pit, and this the elder-tree.

Look, sirs, if you can find the huntsman out

That should have murdered Bassianus here.

  Aaron. My gracious lord, here is the bag of gold.   280

                                [discovers it

Saturninus [*to Titus*]. Two of thy whelps, fell curs
    of bloody kind,

Have here bereft my brother of his life.

Sirs, drag them from the pit unto the prison,

There let them bide until we have devised

Some never-heard-of torturing pain for them.
  Tamora. What, are they in this pit?
    O wondrous thing!
How easily murder is discoveréd!
                         [*they hale them forth*
  Titus. High emperor, upon my feeble knee
I beg this boon, with tears not lightly shed,
290 That this fell fault of my accurséd sons,
Accurséd, if the fault be proved in them—
  Saturninus. If it be proved! you see, it is apparent.
Who found this letter? Tamora, was it you?
  Tamora. Andronicus himself did take it up.
  Titus. I did, my lord, yet let me be their bail,
For by my father's reverend tomb I vow
They shall be ready at your highness' will,
To answer their suspicion with their lives.
  Saturninus. Thou shalt not bail them, see thou
    follow me.
300 Some bring the murdered body, some the murderers,
Let them not speak a word, the guilt is plain,
For by my soul were there worse end than death,
That end upon them should be executed.
  Tamora. Andronicus, I will entreat the king,
Fear not thy sons, they shall do well enough.
  Titus. Come, Lucius, come, stay not to talk
    with them.   [*they go*

[2. 4.] *Enter the Empress' sons with* LAVINIA, *her hands cut off, and her tongue cut out, and ravished*

  Demetrius. So, now go tell, an if thy tongue
    can speak,
Who 'twas that cut thy tongue and ravished thee.
  Chiron. Write down thy mind, bewray thy
    meaning so,

And, if thy stumps will let thee, play the scribe.

Demetrius. See, how with signs and tokens she
  can scrowl.

Chiron. Go home, call for sweet water, wash
  thy hands.

Demetrius. She hath no tongue to call nor hands
  to wash,

And so let's leave her to her silent walks.

Chiron. An 'twere my cause, I should go hang myself.

Demetrius. If thou hadst hands to help thee knit
  the cord.   [*they go* 10

Enter MARCUS from hunting

Marcus. Who is this? my niece, that flies away so fast!
Cousin, a word, where is your husband?

                              [*she turns her face*
If I do dream, would all my wealth would wake me!
If I do wake, some planet strike me down,
That I may slumber an eternal sleep!
Speak, gentle niece, what stern ungentle hands
Hath lopped and hewed and made thy body bare
Of her two branches? those sweet ornaments,
Whose circling shadows kings have sought to sleep in,
And might not gain so great a happiness   20
As half thy love? Why dost not speak to me?
Alas, a crimson river of warm blood,
Like to a bubbling fountain stirred with wind,
Doth rise and fall between thy roséd lips,
Coming and going with thy honey breath.
But, sure, some Tereus hath deflowered thee,
And, lest thou shouldst detect him, cut thy tongue.
Ah, now thou turn'st away thy face for shame!
And, notwithstanding all this loss of blood,
As from a conduit with three issuing spouts,   30

Yet do thy cheeks look red as Titan's face
Blushing to be encountered with a cloud.
Shall I speak for thee? shall I say 'tis so?
O, that I knew thy heart, and knew the beast,
That I might rail at him to ease my mind!
Sorrow concealéd, like an oven stopped,
Doth burn the heart to cinders where it is.
Fair Philomel, why she but lost her tongue,
And in a tedious sampler sewed her mind:
40 But lovely niece, that mean is cut from thee;
A craftier Tereus, cousin, hast thou met,
And he hath cut those pretty fingers off,
That could have better sewed than Philomel.
O, had the monster seen those lily hands
Tremble like aspen leaves upon a lute,
And make the silken strings delight to kiss them,
He would not then have touched them for his life!
Or, had he heard the heavenly harmony
Which that sweet tongue hath made,
50 He would have dropped his knife, and fell asleep
As Cerberus at the Thracian poet's feet.
Come, let us go and make thy father blind,
For such a sight will blind a father's eye.
One hour's storm will drown the fragrant meads,
What will whole months of tears thy father's eyes?
Do not draw back, for we will mourn with thee:
O, could our mourning ease thy misery!   [*they go*

[3. 1.] *Enter the Judges and Senators with Titus' two sons bound, passing on to the place of execution, and* TITUS *going before, pleading*

Titus. Hear me, grave fathers! noble tribunes, stay!
For pity of mine age, whose youth was spent
In dangerous wars, whilst you securely slept;
For all my blood in Rome's great quarrel shed,
For all the frosty nights that I have watched,
And for these bitter tears, which now you see
Filling the agéd wrinkles in my cheeks,
Be pitiful to my condemnéd sons,
Whose souls are not corrupted as 'tis thought.
For two and twenty sons I never wept,   10
Because they died in honour's lofty bed;

Andronicus lieth down and the Judges pass by him

For these, tribunes, in the dust I write
My heart's deep languor and my soul's sad tears:
Let my tears stanch the earth's dry appetite;
My sons' sweet blood will make it shame and blush.
O earth, I will befriend thee more with rain,
That shall distil from these two ancient urns,
Than youthful April shall with all his showers:
In summer's drought I'll drop upon thee still,
In winter with warm tears I'll melt the snow,   20
And keep eternal spring-time on thy face,
So thou refuse to drink my dear sons' blood.

Enter LUCIUS, *with his weapon drawn*

O reverend tribunes! O gentle agéd men!
Unbind my sons, reverse the doom of death,
And let me say, that never wept before,

My tears are now prevailing orators.
Lucius. O noble father, you lament in vain,
The tribunes hear you not, no man is by,
And you recount your sorrows to a stone.
30 *Titus.* Ah, Lucius, for thy brothers let me plead.
Grave tribunes, once more I entreat of you.
Lucius. My gracious lord, no tribune hears you speak.
Titus. Why, 'tis no matter, man, if they did hear
They would not mark me, if they did mark
They would not pity me, yet plead I must,
†And bootless unto them...
Therefore I tell my sorrows to the stones,
Who though they cannot answer my distress,
Yet in some sort they are better than the tribunes,
40 For that they will not intercept my tale:
When I do weep, they humbly at my feet
Receive my tears, and seem to weep with me;
And were they but attiréd in grave weeds,
Rome could afford no tribunes like to these.
A stone is soft as wax, tribunes more hard than stones:
A stone is silent and offendeth not,
And tribunes with their tongues doom men to death.
                                              [*rises*
But wherefore stand'st thou with thy weapon drawn?
Lucius. To rescue my two brothers from their death:
50 For which attempt the judges have pronounced
My everlasting doom of banishment.
Titus. O happy man! they have befriended thee:
Why foolish Lucius, dost thou not perceive
That Rome is but a wilderness of tigers?
Tigers must prey, and Rome affords no prey
But me and mine. How happy art thou then,
From these devourers to be banishéd!
But who comes with our brother Marcus here?

Enter MARCUS with LAVINIA

Marcus. Titus, prepare thy agéd eyes to weep,
Or if not so, thy noble heart to break: 60
I bring consuming sorrow to thine age.
  Titus. Will it consume me? let me see it then.
  Marcus. This was thy daughter.
  Titus.   Why, Marcus, so she is.
  Lucius. Ah me! this object kills me!
  Titus. Faint-hearted boy, arise, and look upon her.
Speak, Lavinia, what accurséd hand
Hath made thee handless in thy father's sight?
What fool hath added water to the sea,
Or brought a faggot to bright-burning Troy?
My grief was at the height before thou cam'st,   70
And now like Nilus it disdaineth bounds.
Give me a sword, I'll chop off my hands too,
For they have fought for Rome, and all in vain;
And they have nursed this woe, in feeding life;
In bootless prayer have they been held up,
And they have served me to effectless use.
Now all the service I require of them
Is, that the one will help to cut the other.
'Tis well, Lavinia, that thou hast no hands,
For hands to do Rome service is but vain.   80
  Lucius. Speak, gentle sister, who hath martyred thee?
  Marcus. O, that delightful engine of her thoughts,
That blabbed them with such pleasing eloquence,
Is torn from forth that pretty hollow cage,
Where like a sweet melodious bird it sung
Sweet varied notes, enchanting every ear!
  Lucius. O, say thou for her, who hath done this deed?
  Marcus. O, thus I found her, straying in the park,
Seeking to hide herself, as doth the deer

90 That hath received some unrecuring wound.
    Titus. It was my dear, and he that wounded her
Hath hurt me more than had he killed me dead:
For now I stand as one upon a rock,
Environed with a wilderness of sea,
Who marks the waxing tide grow wave by wave,
Expecting ever when some envious surge
Will in his brinish bowels swallow him.
This way to death my wretched sons are gone,
Here stands my other son, a banished man,
100 And here my brother weeping at my woes:
But that which gives my soul the greatest spurn
Is dear Lavinia, dearer than my soul.
Had I but seen thy picture in this plight,
It would have madded me: what shall I do
Now I behold thy lively body so?
Thou hast no hands to wipe away thy tears,
Nor tongue to tell me who hath martyred thee:
Thy husband he is dead, and for his death
Thy brothers are condemned, and dead by this.
110 Look, Marcus! ah, son Lucius, look on her!
When I did name her brothers, then fresh tears
Stood on her cheeks, as doth the honey-dew
Upon a gathered lily almost withered.
    Marcus. Perchance she weeps because they killed
      her husband,
Perchance because she knows them innocent.
    Titus. If they did kill thy husband, then be joyful,
Because the law hath ta'en revenge on them.
No, no, they would not do so foul a deed,
Witness the sorrow that their sister makes.
120 Gentle Lavinia, let me kiss thy lips,
Or make some sign how I may do thee ease:
Shall thy good uncle, and thy brother Lucius,

And thou, and I, sit round about some fountain,
Looking all downwards, to behold our cheeks
How they are stained, like meadows yet not dry
With miry slime left on them by a flood?
And in the fountain shall we gaze so long
Till the fresh taste be taken from that clearness,
And made a brine-pit with our bitter tears?
Or shall we cut away our hands, like thine?   130
Or shall we bite our tongues, and in dumb shows
Pass the remainder of our hateful days?
What shall we do? let us, that have our tongues,
Plot some device of further misery,
To make us wondered at in time to come.
  Lucius. Sweet father, cease your tears, for at
     your grief
See how my wretched sister sobs and weeps.
  Marcus. Patience, dear niece. Good Titus, dry
     thine eyes.   [*proffers his handkerchief*
  Titus. Ah, Marcus, Marcus! brother, well I wot
Thy napkin cannot drink a tear of mine,   140
For thou, poor man, hast drowned it with thine own.
  Lucius. Ah, my Lavinia, I will wipe thy cheeks.
     [*proffers his handkerchief; she shakes her head*
  Titus. Mark, Marcus, mark! I understand her signs:
Had she a tongue to speak, now would she say
That to her brother which I said to thee:
His napkin, with his true tears all bewet,
Can do no service on her sorrowful cheeks.
O, what a sympathy of woe is this!
As far from help as Limbo is from bliss!

     Enter AARON the Moor alone

  Aaron. Titus Andronicus, my lord the emperor   150
Sends thee this word, that, if thou love thy sons,

Let Marcius, Lucius, or thyself, old Titus,
Or any one of you, chop off your hand,
And send it to the king: he for the same
Will send thee hither both thy sons alive,
And that shall be the ransom for their fault.
   Titus. O, gracious emperor! O, gentle Aaron!
Did ever raven sing so like a lark,
That gives sweet tidings of the sun's uprise?
160 With all my heart, I'll send the emperor
My hand;
Good Aaron, wilt thou help to chop it off?
   Lucius. Stay, father! for that noble hand of thine,
That hath thrown down so many enemies,
Shall not be sent: my hand will serve the turn.
My youth can better spare my blood than you,
And therefore mine shall save my brothers' lives.
   Marcus. Which of your hands hath not
      defended Rome,
And reared aloft the bloody battle-axe,
170 Writing destruction on the enemy's castle?
O, none of both but are of high desert:
My hand hath been but idle, let it serve
To ransom my two nephews from their death,
Then have I kept it to a worthy end.
   Aaron. Nay, come, agree whose hand shall go along,
For fear they die before their pardon come.
   Marcus. My hand shall go.
   Lucius.   By heaven, it shall not go.
   Titus. Sirs, strive no more; such withered herbs
      as these
Are meet for plucking up, and therefore mine.
180 *Lucius.* Sweet father, if I shall be thought thy son,
Let me redeem my brothers both from death.
   Marcus. And, for our father's sake and mother's care,

Now let me show a brother's love to thee.
Titus. Agree between you, I will spare my hand.
Lucius. Then I'll go fetch an axe.
Marcus. But I will use the axe.

      [*Lucius and Marcus hurry forth*
Titus. Come hither, Aaron. I'll deceive them both;
Lend me thy hand, and I will give thee mine.
(*Aaron.* If that be called deceit, I will be honest,
And never whilst I live deceive men so: 190
But I'll deceive you in another sort,
And that you'll say, ere half an hour pass.

        [*he cuts off Titus' hand*

Enter LUCIUS *and* MARCUS *again*

Titus. Now stay your strife, what shall be
  is dispatched.
Good Aaron, give his majesty my hand,
Tell him it was a hand that warded him
From thousand dangers, bid him bury it—
More hath it merited, that let it have:
As for my sons, say I account of them
As jewels purchased at an easy price,
And yet dear too because I bought mine own. 200
Aaron. I go, Andronicus, and for thy hand
Look by and by to have thy sons with thee.
[*Aside*] Their heads, I mean. O, how this villainy
Doth fat me with the very thoughts of it!
Let fools do good, and fair men call for grace,
Aaron will have his soul black like his face. [*he goes*
 Titus. O, here I lift this one hand up to heaven,
And bow this feeble ruin to the earth.
If any power pities wretched tears,
To that I call! [*to Lavinia*] What, wouldst thou kneel
  with me?   210

Do then, dear heart, for heaven shall hear our prayers,
Or with our sighs we'll breathe the welkin dim,
And stain the sun with fog, as sometime clouds
When they do hug him in their melting bosoms.

Marcus. O brother, speak with possibility,
And do not break into these deep extremes.

Titus. Is not my sorrow deep, having no bottom?
Then be my passions bottomless with them.

Marcus. But yet let reason govern thy lament.

220 *Titus.* If there were reason for these miseries,
Then into limits could I bind my woes:
When heaven doth weep, doth not the earth o'erflow?
If the winds rage, doth not the sea wax mad,
Threat'ning the welkin with his big-swoln face?
And wilt thou have a reason for this coil?
I am the sea; hark, how her sighs doth blow!
She is the weeping welkin, I the earth:
Then must my sea be movéd with her sighs,
Then must my earth with her continual tears

230 Become a deluge, overflowed and drowned:
For why? my bowels cannot hide her woes,
But like a drunkard must I vomit them.
Then give me leave, for losers will have leave
To ease their stomachs with their bitter tongues.

Enter a Messenger, with two heads and a hand

Messenger. Worthy Andronicus, ill art thou repaid
For that good hand thou sent'st the emperor:
Here are the heads of thy two noble sons,
And here's thy hand in scorn to thee sent back,
Thy griefs their sports, thy resolution mocked:

240 That woe is me to think upon thy woes,
More than remembrance of my father's death.

[*he goes*

Marcus. Now let hot Ætna cool in Sicily,
And be my heart an ever-burning hell!
These miseries are more than may be borne!
To weep with them that weep doth ease some deal,
But sorrow flouted at is double death.
  Lucius. Ah, that this sight should make so deep
       a wound,
And yet detested life not shrink thereat!
That ever death should let life bear his name,
Where life hath no more interest but to breathe!   250
                    [*Lavinia kisses Titus*
  Marcus. Alas, poor heart, that kiss is comfortless
As frozen water to a starvéd snake.
  Titus. When will this fearful slumber have an end?
  Marcus. Now, farewell, flattery, die Andronicus,
Thou dost not slumber, see thy two sons' heads,
Thy warlike hand, thy mangled daughter here,
Thy other banished son with this dear sight
Struck pale and bloodless, and thy brother, I,
Even like a stony image cold and numb.
Ah! now no more will I control thy griefs: 260
Rend off thy silver hair, thy other hand
Gnawing with thy teeth, and be this dismal sight
The closing up of our most wretched eyes:
Now is a time to storm, why art thou still?
  Titus. Ha, ha, ha!
  Marcus. Why dost thou laugh? it fits not with
       this hour.
  Titus. Why, I have not another tear to shed;
Besides, this sorrow is an enemy,
And would usurp upon my wat'ry eyes,
And make them blind with tributary tears; .   270
Then which way shall I find Revenge's Cave?
For these two heads do seem to speak to me,

And threat me I shall never come to bliss
Till all these mischiefs be returned again,
Even in their throats that hath committed them.
Come, let me see what task I have to do.
You heavy people, circle me about,
That I may turn me to each one of you,
And swear unto my soul to right your wrongs.

*He kneels, with MARCUS, LUCIUS, LAVINIA and the two
heads round about him; then raises his hand to heaven*

280 The vow is made. [*he rises.*] Come, brother, take
     a head;
And in this hand the other will I bear.
†And Lavinia, thou shalt be employed in this;
Bear thou my hand, sweet wench, between thy teeth:
As for thee, boy, go, get thee from my sight.
Thou art an exile, and thou must not stay.
Hie to the Goths, and raise an army there,
And, if ye love me, as I think you do,
Let's kiss and part, for we have much to do.
     [*they kiss; Titus departs with Marcus and Lavinia*
   Lucius. Farewell, Andronicus, my noble father,
290 The woefull'st man that ever lived in Rome!
Farewell, proud Rome! till Lucius come again,
He leaves his pledges dearer than his life:
Farewell, Lavinia, my noble sister,
O, would thou wert as thou tofore hast been!
But now nor Lucius nor Lavinia lives
But in oblivion and hateful griefs.
If Lucius live, he will requite your wrongs,
And make proud Saturnine and his emperess
Beg at the gates, like Tarquin and his queen.
300 Now will I to the Goths and raise a power,
To be revenged on Rome and Saturnine.   [*he goes*

[3. 2.]   *A room in Titus' house.   A banquet set out*

Enter TITUS, MARCUS, LAVINIA, *and young*
LUCIUS

Titus. So, so, now sit, and look you eat no more
Than will preserve just so much strength in us
As will revenge these bitter woes of ours.
Marcus, unknit that sorrow-wreathen knot:
Thy niece and I, poor creatures, want our hands,
And cannot passionate our tenfold grief
With folded arms. This poor right hand of mine
Is left to tyrannize upon my breast;
Who, when my heart all mad with misery
Beats in this hollow prison of my flesh,   10
Then thus I thump it down.
[*To Lavinia*] Thou map of woe, that thus dost talk
        in signs,
When thy poor heart beats with outrageous beating,
Thou canst not strike it thus to make it still.
Wound it with sighing, girl, kill it with groans;
Or get some little knife between thy teeth,
And just against thy heart make thou a hole,
That all the tears that thy poor eyes let fall
May run into that sink, and soaking in
Drown the lamenting fool in sea-salt tears.   20
   Marcus. Fie, brother, fie! teach her not thus to lay
Such violent hands upon her tender life.
   Titus. How now! has sorrow made thee dote already?
Why, Marcus, no man should be mad but I.
What violent hands can she lay on her life!
Ah, wherefore dost thou urge the name of hands,
To bid Æneas tell the tale twice o'er,

How Troy was burnt and he made miserable?
O, handle not the theme, to talk of hands,
30 Lest we remember still that we have none.
Fie, fie, how franticly I square my talk,
As if we should forget we had no hands,
If Marcus did not name the word of hands!
Come, let's fall to; and, gentle girl, eat this.
Here is no drink? Hark, Marcus, what she says—
I can interpret all her martyred signs—
She says she drinks no other drink but tears,
Brewed with her sorrows, meshed upon her cheeks.
Speechless complainer, I will learn thy thought;
40 In thy dumb action will I be as perfect
As begging hermits in their holy prayers:
Thou shalt not sigh, nor hold thy stumps to heaven,
Nor wink, nor nod, nor kneel, nor make a sign,
But I of these will wrest an alphabet,
And by still practice learn to know thy meaning.
   Boy [*sobs*]. Good grandsire, leave these bitter
     deep laments.
Make my aunt merry with some pleasing tale.
   Marcus. Alas, the tender boy, in passion moved,
Doth weep to see his grandsire's heaviness.
50 *Titus*. Peace, tender sapling, thou art made of tears,
And tears will quickly melt thy life away.
              [*Marcus strikes the dish with a knife*
What dost thou strike at, Marcus, with thy knife?
   Marcus. At that that I have killed, my lord,—a fly.
   Titus. Out on thee, murderer! thou kill'st my heart;
Mine eyes are cloyed with view of tyranny:
A deed of death done on the innocent
Becomes not Titus' brother: get thee gone;
I see thou art not for my company.
   Marcus. Alas, my lord, I have but killed a fly.

Titus. 'But!' How, if that fly had a father
    and mother? 60
How would he hang his slender gilded wings,
And buzz lamenting doings in the air!
Poor harmless fly,
That, with his pretty buzzing melody,
Came here to make us merry! and thou hast killed him.
  Marcus. Pardon me, sir; it was a black ill-favoured fly,
Like to the empress' Moor. Therefore I killed him.
  Titus. O, O, O,
Then pardon me for reprehending thee,
For thou hast done a charitable deed. 70
Give me thy knife, I will insult on him,
Flattering myself, as if it were the Moor,
Come hither purposely to poison me.   [*he strikes at it*
There's for thyself, and that's for Tamora.
Ah, sirrah!
Yet I think we are not brought so low,
But that between us we can kill a fly
That comes in likeness of a coal-black Moor.
  Marcus. Alas, poor man! grief has so wrought on him,
He takes false shadows for true substances. 80
  Titus. Come, take away. Lavinia, go with me:
I'll to thy closet, and go read with thee
Sad stories chancéd in the times of old.
Come, boy, and go with me: thy sight is young,
And thou shalt read when mine begins to dazzle.
                           [*they go*

[4. 1.]   *Before Titus' house*

Enter Lucius' son and LAVINIA *running after him; and
the boy flies from her with his books under his arm. Then
enter* TITUS *and* MARCUS

Boy. Help, grandsire, help! my aunt Lavinia
Follows me everywhere, I know not why.
Good uncle Marcus, see how swift she comes.
Alas, sweet aunt, I know not what you mean.
Marcus. Stand by me, Lucius, do not fear thine aunt.
Titus. She loves thee, boy, too well to do thee harm.
Boy. Ay, when my father was in Rome she did.
Marcus. What means my niece Lavinia by
    these signs?
Titus. Fear her not, Lucius. Somewhat doth
    she mean.
10 See, Lucius, see, how much she makes of thee:
Somewhither would she have thee go with her.
Ah, boy, Cornelia never with more care
Read to her sons than she hath read to thee
Sweet poetry and Tully's Orator.
Canst thou not guess wherefore she plies thee thus?
Boy. My lord, I know not, I, nor can I guess,
Unless some fit or frenzy do possess her:
For I have heard my grandsire say full oft,
Extremity of griefs would make men mad;
20 And I have read that Hecuba of Troy
Ran mad for sorrow. That made me to fear,
Although, my lord, I know my noble aunt
Loves me as dear as e'er my mother did,
And would not, but in fury, fright my youth:
Which made me down to throw my books and fly,
Causeless perhaps. But pardon me, sweet aunt:

And, madam, if my uncle Marcus go,
I will most willingly attend your ladyship.
  Marcus. Lucius, I will.
            [*Lavinia with her stumps turns over the books
               which Lucius has let fall*
  Titus. How now, Lavinia? Marcus, what
       means this?   30
Some book there is that she desires to see:
Which is it, girl, of these? Open them, boy.
But thou art deeper read, and better skilled:
Come, and take choice of all my library,
And so beguile thy sorrow, till the heavens
Reveal the damned contriver of this deed.
Why lifts she up her arms in sequence thus?
  Marcus. I think she means that there were more
       than one
Confederate in the fact. Ay, more there was;
Or else to heaven she heaves them for revenge.   40
  Titus. Lucius, what book is that she tosseth so?
  Boy. Grandsire, 'tis Ovid's Metamorphoses;
My mother gave it me.
  Marcus.   For love of her that's gone,
Perhaps she culled it from among the rest.
  Titus. Soft! so busily she turns the leaves!
Help her!
What would she find? Lavinia, shall I read?
This is the tragic tale of Philomel,
And treats of Tereus' treason and his rape;
And rape, I fear, was root of thy annoy.   50
  Marcus. See, brother, see, note how she quotes
       the leaves.
  Titus. Lavinia, wert thou thus surprised, sweet girl,
Ravished and wronged, as Philomela was,
Forced in the ruthless, vast, and gloomy woods?

See, see!
Ay, such a place there is, where we did hunt,—
O, had we never, never hunted there!—
Patterned by that the poet here describes,
By nature made for murders and for rapes.
60 *Marcus.* O, why should nature build so foul a den,
Unless the gods delight in tragedies?
  Titus. Give signs, sweet girl, for here are none
      but friends,
What Roman lord it was durst do the deed:
Or slunk not Saturnine, as Tarquin erst,
That left the camp to sin in Lucrece' bed?
  Marcus. Sit down, sweet niece: brother, sit down
      by me.
Apollo, Pallas, Jove, or Mercury,
Inspire me, that I may this treason find!
My lord, look here: look here, Lavinia:
70 This sandy plot is plain; guide, if thou canst,
This after me. [*he writes his name with his staff, and
      guides it with feet and mouth.*] I have writ
      my name
Without the help of any hand at all.
Cursed be that heart that forced us to this shift!
Write thou, good niece, and here display at last
What God will have discovered for revenge:
Heaven guide thy pen to print thy sorrows plain,
That we may know the traitors and the truth!
        [*she takes the staff in her mouth, and guides it
          with her stumps and writes*
  Titus. O, do ye read, my lord, what she hath writ?
'Stuprum. Chiron. Demetrius.'
80 *Marcus.* What, what! the lustful sons of Tamora
Performers of this heinous, bloody deed?
  Titus. Magni Dominator poli,

Tam lentus audis scelera? tam lentus vides?
　Marcus. O, calm thee, gentle lord! although I know
There is enough written upon this earth
To stir a mutiny in the mildest thoughts,
And arm the minds of infants to exclaims.
My lord, kneel down with me; Lavinia, kneel;
And kneel, sweet boy, the Roman Hector's hope;
And swear with me, as, with the woful fere　　　　90
And father of that chaste dishonoured dame,
Lord Junius Brutus sware for Lucrece' rape,
That we will prosecute by good advice
Mortal revenge upon these traitorous Goths,
And see their blood, or die with this reproach.
　Titus. 'Tis sure enough, an you knew how,
But if you hurt these bear-whelps, then beware:
The dam will wake; and if she wind ye once,
She's with the lion deeply still in league,
And lulls him whilst she playeth on her back,　　　100
And when he sleeps will she do what she list.
You are a young huntsman, Marcus, let alone;
And, come, I will go get a leaf of brass,
And with a gad of steel will write these words,
And lay it by: the angry northern wind
Will blow these sands like Sibyl's leaves abroad,
And where's our lesson then? Boy, what say you?
　Boy. I say, my lord, that if I were a man,
Their mother's bed-chamber should not be safe
For these base bondmen to the yoke of Rome.　　　110
　Marcus. Ay, that's my boy! thy father hath full oft
For his ungrateful country done the like.
　Boy. And, uncle, so will I, an if I live.
　Titus. Come, go with me into mine armoury:
Lucius, I'll fit thee, and withal my boy
Shall carry from me to the empress' sons

Presents that I intend to send them both:
Come, come; thou'lt do my message, wilt thou not?
   Boy. Ay, with my dagger in their bosoms, grandsire.
120 *Titus.* No, boy, not so; I'll teach thee another course.
Lavinia, come. Marcus, look to my house.
Lucius and I'll go brave it at the court;
Ay, marry, will we, sir; and we'll be waited on.
            [*he goes; Lavinia and young Lucius follow*
   Marcus. O heavens, can you hear a good man groan,
And not relent, or not compassion him?
Marcus, attend him in his ecstasy,
That hath more scars of sorrow in his heart,
Than foe-men's marks upon his battered shield,
But yet so just that he will not revenge.
130 Revenge the heavens for old Andronicus!   [*he goes*

[4. 2.]   *A room in the palace*

*Enter AARON, CHIRON, and DEMETRIUS, at one door:
at another door, young LUCIUS and another, with a
bundle of weapons and verses writ upon them*

   Chiron. Demetrius, here's the son of Lucius,
He hath some message to deliver us.
   Aaron. Ay, some mad message from his
      mad grandfather.
   Boy. My lords, with all the humbleness I may,
I greet your honours from Andronicus.
[*Aside*] And pray the Roman gods confound you both.
   Demetrius. Gramercy, lovely Lucius, what's
      the news?
   (*Boy.* That you are both deciphered, that's the news,
For villains marked with rape. [*aloud*] May it
      please you,

My grandsire, well-advised, hath sent by me　　10
The goodliest weapons of his armoury
To gratify your honourable youth,
The hope of Rome; for so he bade me say;
And so I do, and with his gifts present
Your lordships, that whenever you have need,
You may be arméd and appointed well.
And so I leave you both... [*aside*] like bloody villains.
　　　　　　　　　　　　　　　　　[*he goes*

　Demetrius. What's here? a scroll, and written
　　round about?
Let's see:
'Integer vitæ, scelerisque purus,　　20
Non eget Mauri jaculis, nec arcu.'
　Chiron. O, 'tis a verse in Horace; I know it well:
I read it in the grammar long ago.
　Aaron. Ay, just; a verse in Horace; right, you have it.
[*Aside*] Now, what a thing it is to be an ass!
Here's no sound jest! the old man hath found
　　their guilt,
And sends them weapons wrapped about with lines
That wound, beyond their feeling, to the quick.
But were our witty empress well afoot,
She would applaud Andronicus' conceit.　　30
But let her rest in her unrest awhile.
[*Aloud*] And now, young lords, was't not a happy star
Led us to Rome, strangers, and more than so,
Captives, to be advancéd to this height?
It did me good, before the palace gate
To brave the tribune in his brother's hearing.
　Demetrius. But me more good, to see so great a lord
Basely insinuate and send us gifts.
　Aaron. Had he not reason, lord Demetrius?
Did you not use his daughter very friendly?　　40

Demetrius. I would we had a thousand Roman dames
At such a bay, by turn to serve our lust.
Chiron. A charitable wish and full of love.
Aaron. Here lacks but your mother for to say amen.
Chiron. And that would she for twenty
    thousand more.
Demetrius. Come, let us go, and pray to all the gods
For our belovéd mother in her pains.   [*they make to go*
  (*Aaron.* Pray to the devils, the gods have given us over.
                 [*he stands aside. Trumpets sound*
Demetrius. Why do the emperor's trumpets
    flourish thus?
50 *Chiron.* Belike, for joy the emperor hath a son.
Demetrius. Soft! who comes here?

    *Enter Nurse with a blackamoor child, which seeing
    the young men she hastily covers with her cloak*

Nurse.   Good morrow, lords.
O, tell me, did you see Aaron the Moor?
Aaron [*steps forward*]. Well, more or less, or ne'er
    a whit at all,
Here Aaron is; and what with Aaron now?
Nurse [*weeps*]. O gentle Aaron, we are all undone!
Now help, or woe betide thee evermore!
Aaron. Why, what a caterwauling dost thou keep!
What dost thou wrap and fumble in thy arms?
Nurse. O, that which I would hide from heaven's eye,
60 Our empress' shame and stately Rome's disgrace!
She is delivered, lords, she is delivered.
Aaron. To whom?
Nurse.   I mean, she is brought a-bed.
Aaron. Well, God give her good rest! What hath he
    sent her?
Nurse. A devil.

Aaron.   Why, then she is the devil's dam;
A joyful issue.

Nurse. A joyless, dismal, black, and sorrowful issue!

                              [*shows them the child*

Here is the babe, as loathsome as a toad
Amongst the fair-faced breeders of our clime.
The empress sends it thee, thy stamp, thy seal,
And bids thee christen it with thy dagger's point.   70

Aaron. Zounds, ye whore! is black so base a hue?
Sweet blowse, you are a beauteous blossom, sure.

Demetrius. Villain, what hast thou done?

Aaron. That which thou canst not undo.

Chiron. Thou hast undone our mother.

Aaron. Villain, I have done thy mother.

Demetrius. And therein, hellish dog, thou hast
    undone her.

Woe to her chance, and damned her loathéd choice!
Accursed the offspring of so foul a fiend!

Chiron. It shall not live.   80

Aaron. It shall not die.

Nurse. Aaron, it must; the mother wills it so.

Aaron. What, must it, nurse? then let no man but I
Do execution on my flesh and blood.

Demetrius. I'll broach the tadpole on my
    rapier's point:

Nurse, give it me; my sword shall soon dispatch it.

Aaron. Sooner this sword shall plough thy bowels up.

        [*takes the child from the nurse, and draws*

Stay, murderous villains! will you kill your brother?
Now, by the burning tapers of the sky,
That shone so brightly when this boy was got,   90
He dies upon my scimitar's sharp point
That touches this my first-born son and heir!
I tell you, younglings, not Enceladus,

With all his threat'ning band of Typhon's brood,
Nor great Alcides, nor the god of war,
Shall seize this prey out of his father's hands.
What, what, ye sanguine, shallow-hearted boys!
Ye white-limed walls! ye alehouse painted signs!
Coal-black is better than another hue,
100 In that it scorns to bear another hue;
For all the water in the ocean
Can never turn the swan's black legs to white,
Although she lave them hourly in the flood.
Tell the empress from me, I am of age
To keep mine own, excuse it how she can.

 Demetrius. Wilt thou betray thy noble mistress thus?
 Aaron. My mistress is my mistress, this my self,
The vigour and the picture of my youth:
This before all the world do I prefer;
110 This maugre all the world will I keep safe,
Or some of you shall smoke for it in Rome.

 Demetrius. By this our mother is for ever shamed.
 Chiron. Rome will despise her for this foul escape.
 Nurse. The emperor in his rage will doom her death.
 Chiron. I blush to think upon this ignomy.
 Aaron. Why, there's the privilege your beauty bears:
Fie, treacherous hue! that will betray with blushing
The close enacts and counsels of thy heart!
Here's a young lad framed of another leer:
120 Look, how the black slave smiles upon the father,
As who should say, 'Old lad, I am thine own'.
He is your brother, lords, sensibly fed
Of that self blood that first gave life to you,
And from that womb where you imprisoned were
He is enfranchiséd and come to light:
Nay, he's your brother by the surer side,
Although my seal be stampéd in his face.

Nurse. Aaron, what shall I say unto the empress?
Demetrius. Advise thee, Aaron, what is to be done,
And we will all subscribe to thy advice: 130
Save thou the child, so we may all be safe.
Aaron. Then sit we down and let us all consult.
My son and I will have the wind of you:
Keep there: now talk at pleasure of your safety.

[they sit

Demetrius. How many women saw this child of his?
Aaron. Why, so, brave lords! when we join in league,
I am a lamb: but if you brave the Moor,
The chaféd boar, the mountain lioness,
The ocean swells not so as Aaron storms.
But say again, how many saw the child?   140
Nurse. Cornelia the midwife, and myself,
And no one else but the delivered empress.
Aaron. The emperess, the midwife, and yourself:
Two may keep counsel when the third's away:
Go to the empress, tell her this I said.

[he kills her

Wheak, wheak!
So cries a pig preparéd to the spit.
Demetrius. What mean'st thou, Aaron? wherefore
        didst thou this?
Aaron. O, lord, sir, 'tis a deed of policy!
Shall she live to betray this guilt of ours?   150
A long-tongued babbling gossip? no, lords, no.
And now be it known to you my full intent.
†Not far one Muly lives, my countryman,
His wife but yesternight was brought to bed;
His child is like to her, fair as you are:
Go pack with him, and give the mother gold,
And tell them both the circumstance of all,
And how by this their child shall be advanced,

And be receivéd for the emperor's heir,
160 And substituted in the place of mine,
To calm this tempest whirling in the court;
And let the emperor dandle him for his own.
Hark ye, lords; you see I have given her physic,
                    [*points to the body*
And you must needs bestow her funeral;
The fields are near, and you are gallant grooms.
This done, see that you take no longer days,
But send the midwife presently to me.
The midwife and the nurse well made away,
Then let the ladies tattle what they please.
170 *Chiron.* Aaron, I see, thou wilt not trust the air
With secrets.
    Demetrius.   For this care of Tamora,
Herself and hers are highly bound to thee.
                    [*they bear off the Nurse*
    Aaron. Now to the Goths, as swift as swallow flies,
There to dispose this treasure in mine arms,
And secretly to greet the empress' friends.
Come on, you thick-lipped slave, I'll bear you hence;
For it is you that puts us to our shifts:
I'll make you feed on berries and on roots,
And feed on curds and whey, and suck the goat,
180 And cabin in a cave, and bring you up
To be a warrior and command a camp.   [*he goes*

[4. 3.]   *Before the palace in Rome*

*Enter TITUS, old MARCUS, his son PUBLIUS, young
LUCIUS, and other gentlemen, with bows; and TITUS
bears arrows with letters on the ends of them*

  Titus. Come, Marcus, come; kinsmen, this is the way.
Sir boy, let me see your archery;
Look ye draw home enough, and 'tis there straight.
'Terras Astræa reliquit',
Be you remembered, Marcus: she's gone, she's fled.
Sirs, take you to your tools. You, cousins, shall
Go sound the ocean, and cast your nets;
Haply you may catch her in the sea;
Yet there's as little justice as at land:
No, Publius and Sempronius, you must do it;   10
'Tis you must dig with mattock and with spade,
And pierce the inmost centre of the earth:
Then, when you come to Pluto's region,
I pray you deliver him this petition:
Tell him, it is for justice and for aid,
And that it comes from old Andronicus,
Shaken with sorrows in ungrateful Rome.
Ah, Rome! Well, well; I made thee miserable
What time I threw the people's suffrages
On him that thus doth tyrannize o'er me.   20
Go, get you gone, and pray be careful all,
And leave you not a man of war unsearched:
This wicked emperor may have shipped her hence,
And, kinsmen, then we may go pipe for justice.
  Marcus. O, Publius, is not this a heavy case,
To see thy noble uncle thus distract?
  Publius. Therefore, my lord, it highly us concerns

By day and night t'attend him carefully,
And feed his humour kindly as we may,
30 Till time beget some careful remedy.
   Marcus. Kinsmen, his sorrows are past remedy.
Join with the Goths, and with revengeful war
Take wreak on Rome for this ingratitude,
And vengeance on the traitor Saturnine.
   Titus. Publius, how now! how now, my masters!
What, have you met with her?
   Publius. No, my good lord, but Pluto sends you word,
If you will have revenge from hell, you shall:
Marry, for Justice, she is so employed,
40 He thinks, with Jove in heaven, or somewhere else,
So that perforce you must needs stay a time.
   Titus. He doth me wrong to feed me with delays.
I'll dive into the burning lake below,
And pull her out of Acheron by the heels.
Marcus, we are but shrubs, no cedars we,
No big-boned men framed of the Cyclops' size;
But metal, Marcus, steel to the very back,
Yet wrung with wrongs more than our backs can bear:
And sith there's no justice in earth nor hell,
50 We will solicit heaven, and move the gods
To send down Justice for to wreak our wrongs.
Come, to this gear. You are a good archer, Marcus.
                [*he gives them the arrows, according to the*
                   superscription on the letters
'Ad Jovem', that's for you: here, 'Ad Apollinem':
'Ad Martem', that's for myself:
Here, boy, to Pallas: here, to Mercury:
To Saturn, Caius, not to Saturnine;
You were as good to shoot against the wind.
To it, boy! Marcus, loose when I bid.
Of my word, I have written to effect;

There's not a god left unsolicited.   60
  (*Marcus.* Kinsmen, shoot all your shafts into
        the court:
We will afflict the emperor in his pride.
  Titus. Now, masters, draw. [*they shoot.*] O, well
        said, Lucius!
Good boy, in Virgo's lap; give it Pallas.
  Marcus. My lord, I aimed a mile beyond the moon;
Your letter is with Jupiter by this
  Titus. Ha, ha!
Publius, Publius, what hast thou done!
See, see, thou hast shot off one of Taurus' horns.
  Marcus. This was the sport, my lord: when
        Publius shot,   70
The bull being galled, gave Aries such a knock
That down fell both the Ram's horns in the court,
And who should find them but the empress' villain?
She laughed, and told the Moor he should not choose
But give them to his master for a present.
  Titus. Why, there it goes! God give his lordship joy!

  Enter a Clown, with a basket and two pigeons in it

News, news from heaven! Marcus, the post is come.
Sirrah, what tidings? have you any letters?
Shall I have justice? what says Jupiter?
  Clown. O, the gibbet-maker! he says that he hath 80
taken them down again, for the man must not be hanged
till the next week.
  Titus. But what says Jupiter, I ask thee?
  Clown. Alas, sir, I know not Jubiter; I never drank
with him in all my life.
  Titus. Why, villain, art not thou the carrier?
  Clown. Ay, of my pigeons, sir, nothing else.
  Titus. Why, didst thou not come from heaven?

Clown. From heaven? alas, sir, I never came there!
90 God forbid, I should be so bold to press to heaven in
my young days. Why, I am going with my pigeons to
the tribunal plebs, to take up a matter of brawl betwixt
my uncle and one of the emperal's men.

Marcus. Why, sir, that is as fit as can be to serve for
your oration; and let him deliver the pigeons to the
emperor from you.

Titus. Tell me, can you deliver an oration to the
emperor with a grace?

Clown. Nay, truly, sir, I could never say grace in all
100 my life.

Titus. Sirrah, come hither: make no more ado,
But give your pigeons to the emperor:
By me thou shalt have justice at his hands.
Hold, hold, meanwhile, here's money for thy charges.
Give me a pen and ink.   [*he writes*
Sirrah, can you with a grace deliver a supplication?

Clown. Ay, sir.

Titus. Then here is a supplication for you. And when
you come to him, at the first approach you must kneel,
110 then kiss his foot, then deliver up your pigeons, and
then look for your reward. I'll be at hand, sir! See you
do it bravely.

Clown. I warrant you, sir, let me alone.

Titus. Sirrah, hast thou a knife? come, let me see it.
Here, Marcus, fold it in the oration,
For thou hast made it like an humble suppliant.
And when thou hast given it to the emperor,
Knock at my door, and tell me what he says.

Clown. God be with you, sir; I will.   [*he goes*
120 *Titus.* Come, Marcus, let us go. Publius, follow me.
                              [*they go likewise*

[4. 4.] *Enter Emperor and Empress and her two sons,
with lords, etc. The Emperor brings the arrows in his
hand that Titus shot at him*

  Saturninus. Why, lords, what wrongs are these!
    Was ever seen
An emperor in Rome thus overborne,
Troubled, confronted thus, and for the extent
Of egal justice used in such contempt?
My lords, you know, as know the mightful gods,
However these disturbers of our peace
Buzz in the people's ears, there naught hath passed
But even with law against the wilful sons
Of old Andronicus. And what an if
His sorrows have so overwhelmed his wits,   10
Shall we be thus afflicted in his wreaks,
His fits, his frenzy, and his bitterness?
And now he writes to heaven for his redress!
See, here's to Jove, and this to Mercury,
This to Apollo, this to the god of war:
Sweet scrolls to fly about the streets of Rome!
What's this but libelling against the senate,
And blazoning our unjustice every where?
A goodly humour, is it not, my lords?
As who would say, in Rome no justice were.   20
But if I live, his feignéd ecstasies
Shall be no shelter to these outrages,
But he and his shall know that justice lives
In Saturninus' health; whom, if she sleep,
He'll so awake, as he in fury shall
Cut off the proud'st conspirator that lives.
  Tamora. My gracious lord, my lovely Saturnine,
Lord of my life, commander of my thoughts,
Calm thee, and bear the faults of Titus' age,

30 Th'effects of sorrow for his valiant sons,
Whose loss hath pierced him deep and scarred his heart;
And rather comfort his distresséd plight
Than prosecute the meanest or the best
For these contempts. [*aside*] Why, thus it
    shall become
High-witted Tamora to gloze with all.
But, Titus, I have touched thee to the quick,
Thy life-blood out: if Aaron now be wise,
Then is all safe, the anchor in the port.—

Enter Clown

How now, good fellow? wouldst thou speak with us?
40   *Clown*. Yea, forsooth, an your mistress-ship be em-
perial.
  Tamora. Empress I am, but yonder sits the emperor.
  Clown. 'Tis he. [*kneels*] God and Saint Stephen give
you godden. I have brought you a letter and a couple
of pigeons here.   [*Saturninus reads the letter*
  Saturninus. Go, take him away, and hang
    him presently.
  Clown. How much money must I have?
  Tamora. Come, sirrah, you must be hanged.
  Clown. Hanged! by'r lady, then I have brought up
50 a neck to a fair end.   [*guards lead him away*
  Saturninus. Despiteful and intolerable wrongs!
Shall I endure this monstrous villainy?
I know from whence this same device proceeds.
May this be borne? As if his traitorous sons,
That died by law for murder of our brother,
Have by my means been butchered wrongfully.
Go, drag the villain hither by the hair;
Nor age nor honour shall shape privilege:
For this proud mock I'll be thy slaughterman—

Sly frantic wretch, that holp'st to make me great,   60
In hope thyself should govern Rome and me.

Enter ÆMILIUS, a messenger

What news with thee, Æmilius?
  Æmilius. Arm, arm, my lord! Rome never had
        more cause.
The Goths have gathered head, and with a power
Of high-resolvéd men, bent to the spoil,
They hither march amain, under condúct
Of Lucius, son to old Andronicus;
Who threats, in course of this revenge, to do
As much as ever Coriolanus did.
  Saturninus. Is warlike Lucius general of the Goths? 70
These tidings nip me, and I hang the head
As flowers with frost or grass beat down with storms.
Ay, now begin our sorrows to approach:
'Tis he the common people love so much;
Myself hath often heard them say,
When I have walkéd like a private man,
That Lucius' banishment was wrongfully,
And they have wished that Lucius were
        their emperor.
  Tamora. Why should you fear? is not your
        city strong?
  Saturninus. Ay, but the citizens favour Lucius,   80
And will revolt from me to succour him.
  Tamora. King, be thy thoughts imperious, like
        thy name.
Is the sun dimmed, that gnats do fly in it?
The eagle suffers little birds to sing,
And is not careful what they mean thereby,
Knowing that with the shadow of his wings
He can at pleasure stint their melody:

Even so mayst thou the giddy men of Rome.
Then cheer thy spirit: for know, thou emperor,
90 I will enchant the old Andronicus
With words more sweet, and yet more dangerous,
Than baits to fish, or honey-stalks to sheep;
Whenas the one is wounded with the bait,
The other rotted with delicious feed.
   Saturninus. But he will not entreat his son for us.
   Tamora. If Tamora entreat him, then he will:
For I can smooth, and fill his agéd ears
With golden promises, that, were his heart
Almost impregnable, his old ears deaf,
100 Yet should both ear and heart obey my tongue.
[*To Æmilius*] Go thou before, be our ambassador:
Say that the emperor requests a parley
Of warlike Lucius, and appoint the meeting
Even at his father's house, the old Andronicus.
   Saturninus. Æmilius, do this message honourably,
And if he stand on hostage for his safety,
Bid him demand what pledge will please him best.
   Æmilius. Your bidding shall I do effectually.
                                    [*he goes*

   Tamora. Now will I to that old Andronicus,
110 And temper him with all the art I have,
To pluck proud Lucius from the warlike Goths.
And now, sweet emperor, be blithe again,
And bury all thy fear in my devices.
   Saturninus. Then go successantly, and plead to him.
                                      [*they go*

[5. 1.]   *Plains near Rome*

Enter LUCIUS, with an army of Goths.
Drums and colours

Lucius. Approvéd warriors, and my faithful friends,
I have receivéd letters from great Rome,
Which signifies what hate they bear their emperor,
And how desirous of our sight they are.
Therefore, great lords, be as your titles witness
Imperious, and impatient of your wrongs;
And wherein Rome hath done you any scath,
Let him make treble satisfaction.
 1 Goth. Brave slip, sprung from the great Andronicus,
Whose name was once our terror, now our comfort,   10
Whose high exploits and honourable deeds
Ingrateful Rome requites with foul contempt,
Be bold in us: we'll follow where thou lead'st,
Like stinging bees in hottest summer's day,
Led by their master to the flow'réd fields,
And be avenged on curséd Tamora.
 The other Goths. And as he saith, so say we all
      with him.
 Lucius. I humbly thank him, and I thank you all.
But who comes here, led by a lusty Goth?

Enter a GOTH, leading AARON with his
child in his arms

 2 Goth. Renownéd Lucius, from our troops I strayed 20
To gaze upon a ruinous monastery,
And, as I earnestly did fix mine eye
Upon the wasted building, suddenly
I heard a child cry underneath a wall.
I made unto the noise, when soon I heard

The crying babe controlled with this discourse:
'Peace, tawny slave, half me and half thy dam!
Did not thy hue bewray whose brat thou art,
Had nature lent thee but thy mother's look,
30 Villain, thou mightst have been an emperor:
But where the bull and cow are both milk-white,
They never do beget a coal-black calf.
Peace, villain, peace!'—even thus he rates the babe—
'For I must bear thee to a trusty Goth,
Who, when he knows thou art the empress' babe,
Will hold thee dearly for thy mother's sake.'
With this, my weapon drawn, I rushed upon him,
Surprised him suddenly, and brought him hither,
To use as you think needful of the man.
40 *Lucius.* O worthy Goth, this is the incarnate devil
That robbed Andronicus of his good hand.
This is the pearl that pleased your empress' eye,
And here's the base fruit of her burning lust.
Say, wall-eyed slave, whither wouldst thou convey
This growing image of thy fiend-like face?
Why dost not speak? What, deaf? not a word?
A halter, soldiers! hang him on this tree,
And by his side his fruit of bastardy.
Aaron. Touch not the boy, he is of royal blood.
50 *Lucius.* Too like the sire for ever being good.
First hang the child, that he may see it sprawl—
A sight to vex the father's soul withal.
Get me a ladder.
          [*a ladder brought, and Aaron forced to ascend*
Aaron [*aloft*].   Lucius, save the child;
And bear it from me to the emperess.
If thou do this, I'll show thee wondrous things,
That highly may advantage thee to hear:
If thou wilt not, befall what may befall,

I'll speak no more but 'Vengeance rot you all!'
 Lucius. Say on, and if it please me which
  thou speak'st,
Thy child shall live, and I will see it nourished.   60
 Aaron. And if it please thee! why, assure thee, Lucius,
'Twill vex thy soul to hear what I shall speak;
For I must talk of murders, rapes, and massacres,
Acts of black night, abominable deeds,
Complots of mischief, treason, villainies
Ruthful to hear, yet piteously performed:
And this shall all be buried in my death,
Unless thou swear to me my child shall live.
 Lucius. Tell on thy mind, I say thy child shall live.
 Aaron. Swear that he shall, and then I will begin.   70
 Lucius. Who should I swear by? thou believest
  no god:
That granted, how canst thou believe an oath?
 Aaron. What if I do not? as indeed I do not;
Yet, for I know thou art religious,
And hast a thing within thee calléd conscience,
With twenty popish tricks and ceremonies,
Which I have seen thee careful to observe,
Therefore I urge thy oath; for that I know
An idiot holds his bauble for a god,
And keeps the oath which by that god he swears,   80
To that I'll urge him: therefore thou shalt vow
By that same god, what god soe'er it be,
That thou adorest and hast in reverence,
To save my boy, to nourish and bring him up;
Or else I will discover naught to thee.
 Lucius. Even by my god I swear to thee I will.
 Aaron. First know thou, I begot him on the empress.
 Lucius. O most insatiate and luxurious woman!
 Aaron. Tut, Lucius, this was but a deed of charity

90 To that which thou shalt hear of me anon.
'Twas her two sons that murdered Bassianus;
They cut thy sister's tongue, and ravished her,
And cut her hands, and trimmed her as thou sawest.
   Lucius. O detestable villain! call'st thou
     that trimming?
   Aaron. Why, she was washed, and cut, and trimmed!
     and 'twas
Trim sport for them which had the doing of it.
   Lucius. O barbarous, beastly villains, like thyself!
   Aaron. Indeed, I was their tutor to instruct them.
That codding spirit had they from their mother,
100 As sure a card as ever won the set;
That bloody mind, I think, they learned of me,
As true a dog as ever fought at head.
Well, let my deeds be witness of my worth.
I trained thy brethren to that guileful hole,
Where the dead corpse of Bassianus lay:
I wrote the letter that thy father found,
And hid the gold within that letter mentioned,
Confederate with the queen and her two sons:
And what not done, that thou hast cause to rue,
110 Wherein I had no stroke of mischief in it?
I played the cheater for thy father's hand,
And when I had it drew myself apart,
And almost broke my heart with extreme laughter.
I pried me through the crevice of a wall,
When for his hand he had his two sons' heads;
Beheld his tears and laughed so heartily,
That both mine eyes were rainy like to his:
And when I told the empress of this sport,
She swounded almost at my pleasing tale,
120 And for my tidings gave me twenty kisses.
   Goth. What, canst thou say all this, and never blush?

Aaron. Ay, like a black dog, as the saying is.

Lucius. Art thou not sorry for these heinous deeds?

Aaron. Ay, that I had not done a thousand more.
Even now I curse the day—and yet, I think,
Few come within the compass of my curse—
Wherein I did not some notorious ill:
As kill a man or else devise his death,
Ravish a maid or plot the way to do it,
Accuse some innocent and forswear myself,   130
Set deadly enmity between two friends,
Make poor men's cattle break their necks,
Set fire on barns and hay-stacks in the night,
And bid the owners quench them with their tears.
Oft have I digged up dead men from their graves,
And set them upright at their dear friends' door,
Even when their sorrow almost was forgot,
And on their skins, as on the bark of trees,
Have with my knife carvéd in Roman letters
'Let not your sorrow die, though I am dead.'   140
Tut, I have done a thousand dreadful things
As willingly as one would kill a fly,
And nothing grieves me heartily indeed,
But that I cannot do ten thousand more.

Lucius. Bring down the devil, for he must not die
So sweet a death as hanging presently.

Aaron. If there be devils, would I were a devil,
To live and burn in everlasting fire,
So I might have your company in hell,
But to torment you with my bitter tongue!   150

Lucius. Sirs, stop his mouth, and let him speak
     no more.   [*soldiers gag him and bring him down*

A Goth comes up

Goth. My lord, there is a messenger from Rome

Desires to be admitted to your presence.
Lucius. Let him come near.

Æ<small>MILIUS</small> *is brought forward*

Welcome, Æmilius, what's the news from Rome?
Æmilius. Lord Lucius, and you princes of the Goths,
The Roman emperor greets you all by me;
And, for he understands you are in arms,
He craves a parley at your father's house,
160 Willing you to demand your hostages,
And they shall be immediately delivered.
  1 *Goth.* What says our general?
  Lucius. Æmilius, let the emperor give his pledges
Unto my father and my uncle Marcus,
And we will come. March away.   [*they go*

[5. 2.]   *Court of Titus' house*

Enter T<small>AMORA</small> *and her two sons, disguised*
as Revenge attended by Rape and Murder

  Tamora. Thus, in this strange and sad habiliment,
I will encounter with Andronicus,
And say I am Revenge, sent from below
To join with him and right his heinous wrongs.
Knock at his study, where, they say, he keeps
To ruminate strange plots of dire revenge;
Tell him Revenge is come to join with him,
And work confusion on his enemies.   [*they knock*

T<small>ITUS</small> *opens a window above*

  Titus. Who doth molest my contemplation?
10 Is it your trick to make me ope the door,
That so my sad decrees may fly away,

And all my study be to no effect?
You are deceived: for what I mean to do
See here in bloody lines I have set down.
And what is written shall be executed.

      [he shows a paper written with blood

 Tamora. Titus, I am come to talk with thee.

 Titus. No, not a word. How can I grace my talk,
Wanting a hand to give it action?
Thou hast the odds of me, therefore no more.

 Tamora. If thou didst know me, thou wouldst talk
  with me.   20

 Titus. I am not mad, I know thee well enough.
Witness this wretched stump, witness these
  crimson lines,
Witness these trenches made by grief and care,
Witness the tiring day and heavy night,
Witness all sorrow, that I know thee well
For our proud empress, mighty Tamora:
Is not thy coming for my other hand?

 Tamora. Know thou, sad man, I am not Tamora;
She is thy enemy, and I thy friend.
I am Revenge, sent from th'infernal kingdom 30
To ease the gnawing vulture of thy mind,
By working wreakful vengeance on thy foes.
Come down and welcome me to this world's light;
Confer with me of murder and of death:
There's not a hollow cave or lurking-place,
No vast obscurity or misty vale,
Where bloody murder or detested rape
Can couch for fear, but I will find them out,
And in their ears tell them my dreadful name,
Revenge, which makes the foul offender quake. 40

 Titus. Art thou Revenge? and art thou sent to me,
To be a torment to mine enemies?

Tamora. I am, therefore come down and welcome me.
Titus. Do me some service ere I come to thee.
Lo, by thy side where Rape and Murder stands;
Now give some surance that thou art Revenge,
Stab them, or tear them on thy chariot wheels;
And then I'll come and be thy waggoner,
And whirl along with thee about the globe.
50 Provide two proper palfreys, black as jet,
To hale thy vengeful waggon swift away,
And find out murderers in their guilty caves:
And when thy car is loaden with their heads,
I will dismount, and by thy waggon-wheel
Trot like a servile footman all day long,
Even from Hyperion's rising in the east,
Until his very downfall in the sea.
And day by day I'll do this heavy task,
So thou destroy Rapine and Murder there.
60 *Tamora.* These are my ministers and come with me.
Titus. Are these thy ministers? what are they called?
Tamora. Rape and Murder; therefore calléd so,
'Cause they take vengeance of such kind of men.
Titus. Good Lord, how like the empress' sons
          they are!
And you the empress! but we worldly men
Have miserable, mad, mistaking eyes.
O sweet Revenge, now do I come to thee:
And, if one arm's embracement will content thee,
I will embrace thee in it by and by.
                              [*he shuts the window*
70 *Tamora.* This closing with him fits his lunacy.
Whate'er I forge to feed his brain-sick humours,
Do you uphold and maintain in your speeches,
For now he firmly takes me for Revenge,
And, being credulous in this mad thought,

I'll make him send for Lucius his son;
And, whilst I at a banquet hold him sure,
I'll find some cunning practice out of hand,
To scatter and disperse the giddy Goths,
Or at the least make them his enemies.
See, here he comes, and I must ply my theme.   80

TITUS comes from the house

   Titus. Long have I been forlorn, and all for thee.
Welcome, dread Fury, to my woful house:
Rapine and Murder, you are welcome too:
How like the empress and her sons you are!
Well are you fitted, had you but a Moor:
Could not all hell afford you such a devil?
For well I wot the empress never wags
But in her company there is a Moor;
And, would you represent our queen aright,
It were convenient you had such a devil: 90
But welcome, as you are. What shall we do?
   Tamora. What wouldst thou have us do, Andronicus?
   Demetrius. Show me a murderer, I'll deal with him.
   Chiron. Show me a villain that hath done a rape,
And I am sent to be revenged on him.
   Tamora. Show me a thousand that hath done
      thee wrong,
And I will be revengéd on them all.
   Titus. Look round about the wicked streets of Rome,
And when thou find'st a man that's like thyself,
Good Murder, stab him; he's a murderer.   100
Go thou with him, and when it is thy hap
To find another that is like to thee,
Good Rapine, stab him, he's a ravisher.
Go thou with them, and in the emperor's court
There is a queen attended by a Moor;

Well shalt thou know her by thine own proportion,
For up and down she doth resemble thee;
I pray thee, do on them some violent death;
They have been violent to me and mine.

110 *Tamora.* Well hast thou lessoned us: this shall we do.
But would it please thee, good Andronicus,
To send for Lucius, thy thrice valiant son,
Who leads towards Rome a band of warlike Goths,
And bid him come and banquet at thy house:
When he is here, even at thy solemn feast,
I will bring in the empress and her sons,
The emperor himself, and all thy foes,
And at thy mercy shall they stoop and kneel,
And on them shalt thou ease thy angry heart.
120 What says Andronicus to this device?

Titus. Marcus, my brother! 'tis sad Titus calls.

MARCUS *comes forth*

Go, gentle Marcus, to thy nephew Lucius;
Thou shalt enquire him out among the Goths:
Bid him repair to me and bring with him
Some of the chiefest princes of the Goths:
Bid him encamp his soldiers where they are:
Tell him the emperor and the empress too
Feast at my house, and he shall feast with them.
This do thou for my love, and so let him,
130 As he regards his agéd father's life.

Marcus. This will I do, and soon return again.
[*he goes*

Tamora. Now will I hence about thy business,
And take my ministers along with me.

Titus. Nay, nay, let Rape and Murder stay with me,
Or else I'll call my brother back again,
And cleave to no revenge but Lucius.

(*Tamora.* What say you, boys? will you abide
 with him,
Whiles I go tell my lord the emperor
How I have governed our determined jest?
Yield to his humour, smooth and speak him fair, 140
And tarry with him till I turn again.
 (*Titus.* I knew them all, though they supposed
 me mad;
And will o'er-reach them in their own devices,
A pair of cursèd hell-hounds and their dam.
 Demetrius. Madam, depart at pleasure, leave us here.
 Tamora. Farewell, Andronicus: Revenge now goes
To lay a complot to betray thy foes.
 Titus. I know thou dost; and, sweet
  Revenge, farewell.   [*she goes*
 Chiron. Tell us, old man, how shall we be employed?
 Titus. Tut, I have work enough for you to do. 150
Publius, come hither, Caius, and Valentine!

   PUBLIUS and others come from the house

 Publius. What is your will?
 Titus. Know you these two?
 Publius. The empress' sons, I take them, Chiron
and Demetrius.
 Titus. Fie, Publius, fie! thou art too much deceived;
The one is Murder, and Rape is the other's name:
And therefore bind them, gentle Publius:
Caius and Valentine, lay hands on them:
Oft have you heard me wish for such an hour, 160
And now I find it: therefore bind them sure;
And stop their mouths, if they begin to cry.
            [*he goes in*
  [*Publius, &c. lay hold on Chiron and Demetrius*
 Chiron. Villains, forbear! we are the empress' sons.

Publius. And therefore do we what we
        are commanded.
Stop close their mouths, let them not speak a word:
Is he sure bound? look that you bind them fast.

*Enter TITUS ANDRONICUS with a knife,
        and LAVINIA with a basin*

Titus. Come, come, Lavinia; look, thy foes are bound.
Sirs, stop their mouths, let them not speak to me,
But let them hear what fearful words I utter.
170 O villains, Chiron and Demetrius!
Here stands the spring whom you have stained
        with mud,
This goodly summer with your winter mixed.
You killed her husband, and, for that vile fault
Two of her brothers were condemned to death,
My hand cut off and made a merry jest:
Both her sweet hands, her tongue, and that more dear
Than hands or tongue, her spotless chastity,
Inhuman traitors, you constrained and forced.
What would you say, if I should let you speak?
180 Villains, for shame you could not beg for grace.
Hark, wretches, how I mean to martyr you.
This one hand yet is left to cut your throats,
Whiles that Lavinia 'tween her stumps doth hold
The basin that receives your guilty blood.
You know your mother means to feast with me,
And calls herself Revenge, and thinks me mad:
Hark, villains, I will grind your bones to dust,
And with your blood and it I'll make a paste,
And of the paste a coffin I will rear,
190 And make two pasties of your shameful heads,
And bid that strumpet, your unhallowed dam,
Like to the earth, swallow her own increase.

This is the feast that I have bid her to,
And this the banquet she shall surfeit on;
For worse than Philomel you used my daughter,
And worse than Progne I will be revenged.
And now prepare your throats. Lavinia, come,
Receive the blood; and when that they are dead,
Let me go grind their bones to powder small,
And with this hateful liquor temper it,　　　　　200
And in that paste let their vile heads be baked.
Come, come, be every one officious
To make this banquet, which I wish may prove
More stern and bloody than the Centaurs' feast.

                  [he cuts their throats

So, now bring them in, for I'll play the cook,
And see them ready against their mother comes.

                [they bear the bodies into the house

[5. 3.] *Enter* LUCIUS, MARCUS, *and the Goths, with* AARON *a prisoner, and the child in the arms of an attendant*

Lucius. Uncle Marcus, since 'tis my father's mind
That I repair to Rome, I am content.
　1 *Goth.* And ours with thine, befall what
　　　fortune will.
Lucius. Good uncle, take you in this barbarous Moor,
This ravenous tiger, this accursèd devil;
Let him receive no sustenance, fetter him,
Till he be brought unto the empress' face,
For testimony of her foul proceedings:
And see the ambush of our friends be strong;
I fear the emperor means no good to us.　　　　10
　Aaron. Some devil whisper curses in my ear,
And prompt me, that my tongue may utter forth
The venomous malice of my swelling heart!

Lucius. Away, inhuman dog! unhallowed slave!
Sirs, help our uncle to convey him in.

> [*Goths lead Aaron in. Trumpets sound*

The trumpets show the emperor is at hand.

*Enter Emperor and Empress, with Tribunes
and others*

Saturninus. What, hath the firmament mo suns
than one?
Lucius. What boots it thee to call thyself a sun?
Marcus. Rome's emperor, and nephew, break
the parle;
20 These quarrels must be quietly debated.
The feast is ready, which the careful Titus
Hath ordained to an honourable end,
For peace, for love, for league, and good to Rome.
Please you, therefore, draw nigh, and take your places.
Saturninus. Marcus, we will.

*Servants bring forth a table. Trumpets sounding, enter
TITUS, like a cook, placing the dishes, and LAVINIA with
a veil over her face, young LUCIUS, and others*

Titus. Welcome, my lord; welcome, dread queen;
Welcome, ye warlike Goths; welcome, Lucius;
And welcome, all: although the cheer be poor,
'Twill fill your stomachs; please you eat of it.
30 *Saturninus.* Why art thou thus attired, Andronicus?
Titus. Because I would be sure to have all well,
To entertain your highness and your empress.
Tamora. We are beholding to you, good Andronicus.
Titus. An if your highness knew my heart, you were.
My lord the emperor, resolve me this:
Was it well done of rash Virginius
To slay his daughter with his own right hand,

Because she was enforced, stained, and deflowered?
  Saturninus. It was, Andronicus.
  Titus. Your reason, mighty lord!   40
  Saturninus. Because the girl should not survive
      her shame,
And by her presence still renew his sorrows.
  Titus. A reason mighty, strong, and effectual,
A pattern, precedent, and lively warrant,
For me, most wretched, to perform the like.
Die, die, Lavinia, and thy shame with thee,
And with thy shame thy father's sorrow die!

                              [*he kills her*

  Saturninus. What hast thou done, unnatural
      and unkind?
  Titus. Killed her for whom my tears have made
      me blind.
I am as woful as Virginius was,   50
And have a thousand times more cause than he
To do this outrage, and it now is done.
  Saturninus. What, was she ravished? tell who did
      the deed.
  Titus. Will't please you eat? will't please your
      highness feed?
  Tamora. Why hast thou slain thine only
      daughter thus?
  Titus. Not I; 'twas Chiron and Demetrius:
They ravished her and cut away her tongue;
And they, 'twas they, that did her all this wrong.
  Saturninus. Go, fetch them hither to us presently.
  Titus. Why, there they are both, bakéd in this pie, 60
Whereof their mother daintily hath fed,
Eating the flesh that she herself hath bred.
'Tis true, 'tis true; witness my knife's sharp point.

                              [*he stabs the empress*

Saturninus. Die, frantic wretch, for this accurséd deed.
                                                    [*kills Titus*
Lucius. Can the son's eye behold his father bleed?
There's meed for meed, death for a deadly deed.

He kills Saturninus. A great tumult. Lucius, Marcus,
and others go up into the balcony

  Marcus. You sad-faced men, people and sons of Rome,
By uproars severed, as a flight of fowl
Scattered by winds and high tempestuous gusts,
70 O, let me teach you how to knit again
This scattered corn into one mutual sheaf,
These broken limbs again into one body;
Lest Rome herself be bane unto herself,
And she whom mighty kingdoms curt'sy to,
Like a forlorn and desperate castaway,
Do shameful execution on herself.
But if my frosty signs and chaps of age,
Grave witnesses of true experience,
Cannot induce you to attend my words,—
[*to Lucius*] Speak, Rome's dear friend, as erst
80   our ancestor,
When with his solemn tongue he did discourse
To love-sick Dido's sad attending ear
The story of that baleful burning night,
When subtle Greeks surprised King Priam's Troy;
Tell us what Sinon hath bewitched our ears,
Or who hath brought the fatal engine in
That gives our Troy, our Rome, the civil wound.
My heart is not compact of flint nor steel;
Nor can I utter all our bitter grief,
90 But floods of tears will drown my oratory,
And break my utt'rance, even in the time
When it should move ye to attend me most,
And force you to commiseration.

Here's Rome's young captain, let him tell the tale,
While I stand by and weep to hear him speak.
  Lucius. Then, gracious auditory, be it known to you,
That Chiron and the damned Demetrius
Were they that murderéd our emperor's brother;
And they it were that ravishéd our sister.
For their fell faults our brothers were beheaded,   100
Our father's tears despised, and basely cozened
Of that true hand that fought Rome's quarrel out
And sent her enemies unto the grave.
Lastly, myself unkindly banishéd,
The gates shut on me, and turned weeping out,
To beg relief among Rome's enemies;
Who drowned their enmity in my true tears,
And oped their arms to embrace me as a friend:
I am the turned-forth, be it known to you,
That have preserved her welfare in my blood,   110
And from her bosom took the enemy's point,
Sheathing the steel in my advent'rous body.
Alas, you know I am no vaunter, I;
My scars can witness, dumb although they are,
That my report is just and full of truth.
But, soft! methinks, I do digress too much,
Citing my worthless praise. O, pardon me,
For when no friends are by, men praise themselves.
  Marcus. Now is my turn to speak. Behold the child:
                                                  [*points*
Of this was Tamora deliveréd,   120
The issue of an irreligious Moor,
Chief architect and plotter of these woes:
The villain is alive in Titus' house,
†Damned as he is, to witness this is true.
Now judge what cause had Titus to revenge
These wrongs, unspeakable, past patience,

Or more than any living man could bear.
Now have you heard the truth. What say you, Romans?
Have we done aught amiss, show us wherein,
130 And, from the place where you behold us pleading
The poor remainder of Andronici
Will, hand in hand, all headlong hurl ourselves
And on the ragged stones beat forth our souls,
And make a mutual closure of our house.
Speak, Romans, speak, and if you say we shall,
Lo, hand in hand, Lucius and I will fall.
　　Æmilius. Come, come, thou reverend man of Rome,
And bring our emperor gently in thy hand,
Lucius our emperor; for well I know
140 The common voice do cry it shall be so.
　　All. Lucius, all hail, Rome's royal emperor!
　　Marcus [to soldiers]. Go, go into old Titus'
　　　　sorrowful house,
And hither hale that misbelieving Moor,
To be adjudged some direful slaught'ring death,
As punishment for his most wicked life.

　　　LUCIUS, MARCUS, and the others descend

　　All. Lucius, all hail, Rome's gracious governor!
　　Lucius. Thanks, gentle Romans: may I govern so,
To heal Rome's harms and wipe away her woe!
But, gentle people, give me aim awhile,
150 For nature puts me to a heavy task.
Stand all aloof; but, uncle, draw you near,
To shed obsequious tears upon this trunk.
　　　　　　　　　　　[he kisses the dead Titus
O, take this warm kiss on thy pale cold lips,
These sorrowful drops upon thy blood-stained face,
The last true duties of thy noble son!
　　Marcus. Tear for tear and loving kiss for kiss

Thy brother Marcus tenders on thy lips:
O, were the sum of these that I should pay
Countless and infinite, yet would I pay them!
  Lucius. Come hither, boy; come, come, and
      learn of us   160
To melt in showers: thy grandsire loved thee well:
Many a time he danced thee on his knee,
Sung thee asleep, his loving breast thy pillow;
Many a story hath he told to thee,
And bid thee bear his pretty tales in mind,
And talk of them when he was dead and gone.
  Marcus. How many thousand times hath these
      poor lips,
When they were living, warmed themselves on thine!
O, now, sweet boy, give them their latest kiss.
Bid him farewell; commit him to the grave;   170
Do him that kindness, and take leave of him.
  Boy. O, grandsire, grandsire! even with all my heart
Would I were dead, so you did live again!—
O Lord, I cannot speak to him for weeping,
My tears will choke me, if I ope my mouth.

Soldiers return with AARON

  Roman. You sad Andronici, have done with woes;
Give sentence on this execrable wretch,
That hath been breeder of these dire events.
  Lucius. Set him breast-deep in earth, and
      famish him;
There let him stand and rave and cry for food: 180
If any one relieves or pities him,
For the offence he dies. This is our doom.
Some stay, to see him fastened in the earth.
  Aaron. Ah, why should wrath be mute, and
      fury dumb?

I am no baby, I, that with base prayers
I should repent the evils I have done:
Ten thousand worse than ever yet I did
Would I perform, if I might have my will:
If one good deed in all my life I did,
190 I do repent it from my very soul.
　　Lucius. Some loving friends convey the
　　　　emperor hence,
And give him burial in his father's grave:
My father and Lavinia shall forthwith
Be closéd in our household's monument.
As for that ravenous tiger, Tamora,
No funeral rite, nor man in mourning weed,
No mournful bell shall ring her burial;
But throw her forth to beasts and birds of prey.
Her life was beastly and devoid of pity,
200 And being dead, let birds on her take pity.　　*[they go*

GLOSSARY

GLOSSARY

ABJECTLY, meanly, with contempt; 2. 3. 4

ABUSE, deceive; 2. 3. 87

ACCITE (cf. *2 Hen. IV*, 2. 2. 58; 5. 2. 141), summon; 1. 1. 27

ACHERON, one of the rivers of Hades here supposed a lake, (cf. note 3. 5. 15, *Macb.*); 4. 3. 44

ACHIEVE, gain, obtain; 2. 1. 80, 81

ACTÆON, hunter turned into a stag and torn to pieces by his own hounds as a punishment for gazing on Diana bathing; 2. 3. 63

ADMIT, favour, declare for (cf. *K. John*, 2. 1. 361; *Cor.* 2. 3. 151); 1. 1. 222

ADVICE, deliberation; 1. 1. 379; 4. 1. 93

ADVISE, consider, bethink oneself (cf. *well-advised*); 4. 2. 129

AFFECT, (i) love; 2. 1. 28; (ii) aim at; 2. 1. 105.

AFFY, (in) trust (v. note); 1. 1. 47

AFOOT, 'up and about', after illness or childbirth; 4. 2. 29

AIM, 'give aim' = 'guide (a person) in his aim by informing him of the result of a preceding shot' (O.E.D.), and so (perhaps) fig. 'give room and scope to his thoughts' (Schmidt); 5. 3. 149

ALCIDES, name of Hercules, as descendant of Alcaeus; 4. 2. 95

AMAIN, with speed; 4. 4. 66

ANCHORAGE, 'set of anchors' (O.E.D.); 1. 1. 73

ANNOY (sb.), harm, injury (here in strong sense); 4. 1. 50

ANSWER, (i) (*a*) render account for, bear responsibility for; (*b*) pay for; 1. 1. 412, 2. 3. 298; (ii) respond to; 3. 1. 38

APPARENT, manifest; 2. 3. 292

APPOINT, equip; 4. 2. 16

APPROVE, prove; 2. 1. 35; 5. 1. 1

ARM (fig.), make strong; 4. 1. 87

ASPIRED, risen, attained; 1. 1. 177

ASTRÆA, goddess of justice who lived on earth in the Golden Age, and retired to Heaven in the Age of Iron; 4. 3. 4

BANDY, brawl, fight (cf. *Rom.* 3. 1. 92); 1. 1. 312

BAUBLE, the court fool's stick with top carved in shape of head; 5. 1. 79

BAY (hunting term), (i) 'deep, prolonged barking of hounds' (Onions); 2. 2. 3; (ii) position of hunted animal when it turns and faces the hounds ('at a bay', 'at the bay'), extremity; 4. 2. 42

BEHOLDING, beholden, under obligation (freq. in Sh.); 1. 1. 396; 5. 3. 33

BENT TO, intent upon; 4. 4. 65

BERAY, foul, defile (cf. Holinshed, *Hist. Scot.* ii. 150, 'the bed all beraied with blood'); 2. 3. 222

BETRAY, deceive, entrap (cf.
Oth. 5. 2. 6); 5. 2. 147

BITE ONE'S TONGUE, be silent
or speechless (cf. 2 Hen. VI,
1. 1. 230; 3 Hen. VI, 1. 4.
47); 3. 1. 131

BLAZON, proclaim; 4. 4. 18

BLOWSE, 'ruddy-faced fat
wench' (Schmidt), here of
a baby boy (v. note); 4. 2. 72

BOAST (sb.), display (cf. vb.
Lucr. l. 55); 2. 3. 11

BOLD IN, confident in; 5. 1. 13

BOOTY, prey, victims (of a
robbery) (cf. 3 Hen. VI,
1. 4. 63); 2. 3. 49

BOWELS, lit. and fig. as seat of
affections; 3. 1. 231

BRABBLE, brawl, quarrel; 2. 1.
62

BRAVE (sb.), bravado, threat;
2. 1. 30

BRAVE (vb.), (i) challenge, defy;
2. 1. 25 S.D.; 2. 3. 126;
4. 2. 36, 137; (ii) 'brave it'
= defiantly show oneself;
4. 1. 122

BRAVE (adj.), epithet of praise
with vague sense, 'fine';
4. 2. 136

BRAWL, quarrel; 4. 3. 92

BREAK, (i) (into), speak passionately or impulsively (cf.
mod. 'break out into'); 3. 1.
216; (ii) (tr.) 'break one's
heart' = die (cf. M.W.W.
2. 2. 284); 5. 1. 113;
(iii) interrupt; 5. 3. 19, 91

BREATHE DIM, make dim with
one's breath; 3. 1. 212

BRINISH, briny; 3. 1. 97

BROACH, (i) (a quarrel), begin,
enter on; 2. 1. 67; (ii) stick
on a sword's point as on a
spit (cf. Hen. V, 5 Pr. 32);
4. 2. 85

BUSINESS, trouble (O.E.D. 7);
1. 1. 192

BUZZ, whisper (scandal, etc.)
into someone's ear (cf.
'buzzer', Ham. 4. 5. 89);
4. 4. 7

CABIN (vb.), lodge in a con-
fined space (cf. Macb. 3. 4.
24); 4. 2. 180

CANDIDATUS, candidate for
office in Rome (lit. one
clothed in white); 1. 1. 185

CAPITOL, Hist. the hill N.W.
of the Forum on which stood
the temple of Jupiter Capito-
linus. Usually identified with
the Senate House by the
Elizabethans; 1. 1. 12, 77.

CARD, v. sure card; 5. 1. 100

CAREFUL, costing or taking
trouble; 4. 3. 30; 5. 3. 21

CARRY, carry on or off, 'get
away with'; 2. 3. 127

CASTLE (fig.), defensive strong-
hold; 3. 1. 170

CAUSE, (a) case, affair, (b)
disease, sickness; 2. 4. 9

CAUSELESS (adv.), without rea-
sonable cause; 4. 1. 26

CENTAURS' FEAST. Refers to
the bloody battle which followed the marriage feast to
which the Lapithae invited
the Centaurs; 5. 2. 204

CERTAIN, sure; 2. 1. 95

CHAFED, brought to bay (freq.);
4. 2. 138

CHALLENGE, accuse (cf. Macb.
3. 4. 42); 1. 1. 340.

CHAMPION, warrior, man of
valour (elsewhere in this
sense only in 1, 2, 3 Hen. VI);
1. 1. 65, 151

CHANCE, mishap; 4. 2. 78

CHARGE, expense; 4. 3. 104

CHARMING, (a) attractive, (b) binding with a magic spell; 2. 1. 16

CHASE, hunting-ground; 2. 2. 21; 2. 3. 255

CHEATER, officer appointed to look after property forfeited to the Crown (escheats); hence, because of his opportunities of fraud, fig. in the modern sense; 5. 1. 111

CHEER, (i) look, countenance; 1. 1. 264; (ii) hospitable fare; 5. 3. 28

CIMMERIAN, 'black man', from Cimmerians in Homer, on whose land the sun never shone, and hence a symbol for darkness; 2. 3. 72

CIRCUMSCRIBE, confine within limits, restrain; 1. 1. 68

CITE, make mention of; 5. 3. 117

CIVIL, belonging to civil strife; 5. 3. 87

CLEANLY, at once 'cleverly' and 'completely'; 2. 1. 94

CLEARNESS, (a) (abstr. for concr.) clear pool, (b) purity (cf. All's Well, 1. 3. 6); 3. 1. 128

CLOSE, enclose; 5. 3. 194

CLOSING (sb.), agreement, coming to terms; 5. 2. 70

CLOSURE, end; 5. 3. 134

CLUBS, cry to summon aid to stop a brawl in London (v. note); 2. 1. 37

COACH, chariot; 2. 1. 7

COCYTUS, one of the rivers of Hades, here used for Hades itself (v. note); 2. 3. 236

CODDING, lustful (here only), from 'cods' = testicles (O.E.D. 'cod' 4); 5. 1. 99

COFFIN, pie-crust (cf. 'custard-coffin'; Shrew, 4. 3. 82); 5. 2. 189

COIL, fuss, commotion; 3. 1. 225

COIN (vb.), produce (fig. from minting a coin); 2. 3. 5

COMPACT (adj.), composed (cf. M.N.D. 5. 1. 8); 5. 3. 88

COMPETITOR. (In Sh. usu. = partner.) (i) candidate; 1. 1. 63; (ii) rival; 2. 1. 77

COMPLAINER, mourner, lamenter; 3. 2. 39

COMPLOT, plot; 2. 3. 265; 5. 1. 65; 5. 2. 147

CONCEIT, device, invention; 4. 2. 30

CONDUCT, leadership, command; 4. 4. 66

CONFEDERATE (sb. and adj.), conspirator, joined in conspiracy (cf. Ham. 3. 2. 256, 'confederate season'); 1. 1. 303, 344; 4. 1. 39; 5. 1. 108

CONFIDENT, confiding, trustful; 1. 1. 61

CONFLICT, used equivocally of sexual intercourse; 2. 3. 21

CONFOUND, ruin, destroy; 4. 2. 6

CONFRONT, face as accuser or witness (O.E.D. 3b.); 4. 4. 3

CONFUSION, ruin, destruction; 2. 3. 184; 5. 2. 8

CONTROL, thwart, overrule, restrain; 1. 1. 420; 3. 1. 260; check; 5. 1. 26

CONTROLMENT, check, restraint; 2. 1. 68

CONVENIENT, fitting, proper; 5. 2. 90

CORDIAL (source of) comfort; 1. 1. 166

CORNELIA (v. note); 4. 1. 12

COUCH, lie hidden; 5. 2. 38

COURT IT, woo; 2. 1. 93

COUSIN, niece (in Sh. of any
near relation); 2. 4. 12, 41

COZEN, cheat; 5. 3. 101

CRACK, explosive noise (of gun,
thunder, etc.) (cf. *Macb.*
4. 1. 117); 2. 1. 3

CREST. As a symbol of military
honour here = 'honour'; 1.
1. 364

CROSS, perverse; 2. 3. 53

CRY, deep barking of hounds in
unison; 2. 2. 10 (S.D.)

CURTAIN, cover, conceal; 2. 3.
24

CUT, (i) cut off; 2. 4. 2, 27;
3. 1. 78 *et al.*; (ii) take away
(w. quibble on (i)); 2. 4. 40

CYCLOPS, race of one-eyed
giants in Homer and Hesiod;
4. 3. 46

DAINTILY, deliciously (w.
ironical quibble on sense,
'fastidiously'); 5. 3. 61

DAINTY, delicate, lovely; 2. 1.
117

DANCING-RAPIER, sword worn
only for ornament in dancing
(cf. *All's Well*, 2. 1. 32–3);
2. 1. 39

DATE, term of existence (cf.
M.N.D. 3. 2. 373, etc.);
1. 1. 168

DAYS (see note); 4. 2. 166

DAZZLE (of the eyes), lose
clearness of sight (cf. *3 Hen.
VI*, 2. 1. 25; Webster,
Duch. of Malfi, 4. 2. 281);
3. 2. 85

DEADLY-STANDING, fixed in a
deathlike stare; 2. 3. 32

DEAL, 'some deal' = a little;
3. 1. 245

DEAR, (i) (*a*) precious, beloved,
(*b*) expensive; 3. 1. 200;
(ii) grievous, dire (freq. in

Sh., a different word from
(i)); 3. 1. 257

DECIPHER, detect (cf. *1 Hen.
VI*, 4. 1. 184); 4. 2. 8

DECREE, (vb.) resolve; 2. 3.
274

DECREE (sb.) decision; 5. 2. 11

DESERT, merit, meritorious
deed; 1. 1. 24, 45, 236, 256;
3. 1. 170

DETECT, expose; 2. 4. 27

DETESTED, detestable; 2. 3. 93

DEVICE, (i) contrivance, plot;
1. 1. 395; (ii) plan; 2. 1.
79; 3. 1. 134; 4. 4. 53, 113;
5. 2. 120, 143

DEVISE, plot; 5. 1. 128

DIGRESS, transgress, offend
(cf. *Ric. II*, 5. 3. 66); 5. 3.
116

DISCOVER, reveal (most freq.
Sh. sense); 4. 1. 75; 5. 1. 85

DISTRACT, distraught; 4. 3. 26

DO, have sexual intercourse
with; 4. 2. 76

DOMINATOR. '(Astrol.) A planet
or sign supposed to dominate
a particular person' (O.E.D.);
2. 3. 31

DOOM, pronounce judgement
(rare sense in Sh., but cf.
Cym. 5. 5. 420); 4. 2. 114

DOUBT, suspect; 2. 3. 68

DOWNFALL, (sun's) setting;
5. 2. 57

DRIVE (upon), set (on), rush
(upon). A hunting term
(v. Madden, p. 321); 2. 3. 64

DRUG, plant from which poison
can be extracted; 1. 1. 154

DULL, gloomy, dark; 2. 1. 128

EASE, 'do ease' = bring relief
from sorrow; 3. 1. 121

ECSTASY, madness, fit of madness; 4. 1. 126; 4. 4. 21

EGAL, equal (cf. *Merch.* 3. 4. 13); 4. 4. 4

EMPERAL, EMPERIAL, blunder for 'emperor'; 4. 3. 93; 4. 4. 40–1

EMPERY, (i) dominion; 1. 1. 19 (cf. *Hen. V*, 1. 2. 227); (ii) status of emperor; 1. 1. 22, 201

EMPIRE, status of emperor; 1. 1. 183

ENACT (sb.), purpose; 4. 2. 118

ENCELADUS, one of the Titans who warred against the Olympian gods; 4. 2. 93

ENGINE, lit. mother wit (> Lat. *ingenium*), (i) scheme; 2. 1. 123; (ii) instrument (cf. 'engine of thoughts', *V.A.* l. 367); 3. 1. 82; (i) and (ii) app. combined in 5. 3. 86

ENSIGN, token, emblem; 1. 1. 252

ENTRAILS, inward parts, interior (v. note ll. 226–30); 2. 3. 230

ENTREAT, entreaty; 1. 1. 449, 483

ENVIOUS, malicious, malignant; 3. 1. 96

ENVY, hatred, malice; 2. 1. 4

ESCAPE (or 'scape'), transgression, esp. sexual (cf. *Oth.* 1. 3. 197; *W.T.* 3. 3. 71, 72); 4. 2. 113

EXCLAIM (sb.), outcry, protest (cf. *Ric. II*, 1. 2. 2; *Ric. III*, 1. 2. 52; 4. 4. 135); 4. 1. 87

EXTENT, 'exercise (of justice, kindness)' (Onions); 4. 4. 3

EXTREMES, extravagant passion or hysterical behaviour (cf. *W.T.* 4. 4. 6; *Shrew*, Ind. i. 137); 3. 1. 216

FAIR (adv.), civilly, courteously (cf. *Ric. III*, 4. 4. 151); 1. 1. 46; 5. 2. 140

FAT, fig. = 'delight'; 3. 1. 204

FATAL-PLOTTED, contrived so as to cause a death (here only); 2. 3. 47

FEAR (vb.), fear for; 2. 3. 305

FEELING, effect upon the feeling or senses (cf. *Ric. II*, 1. 3. 301); 4. 2. 28

FERE, spouse (only *Per.* Pr. l. 21 elsewhere in Sh.); 4. 1. 90

FIND, (i) experience; 2. 3. 150; 5. 2. 161; (ii) find out; 4. 2. 26

FIT (sb.), paroxysm (of lust); 2. 1. 134; (of madness); 4. 1. 17; 4. 4. 12

FIT (vb.) furnish (a person) with (something); 4. 1. 115; 5. 2. 85

FLATTER, deceive; 3. 2. 72

FLATTERY, delusion, self-deception; 3. 1. 254

FLEECE, mass of hair on the head (cf. *Scn.* 68. 8); 2. 3. 34

FOLD, conceal (cf. *Lucr.* l. 1073); 2. 3. 266

FOOL, a term of endearment or pity (cf. *Tw. Nt* 5. 1. 369; *Lear*, 5. 3. 305); 3. 2. 20

FORFEND, avert, forbid; 1. 1. 434

FORGE, invent; 5. 2. 71

FORLORN, of wretched appearance; 2. 3. 94

FORWARD, ardent, eager; 1. 1. 56

FRANKLY, bounteously, generously; 1. 1. 420

FRANTIC, mad; 4. 4. 60; 5. 3. 64

FRANTICLY, like a madman; 3. 2. 31

FRAUGHT (sb.), freight; 1. 1. 71

FUMBLE, 'wrap up clumsily' (O.E.D. 3); 4. 2. 58

FURY, madness; 4. 1. 24

GAD, sharp spike; 'gad of steel' = stylus (cf. O.E.D.); 4. 1. 104

GEAR, business; 4. 3. 52

GENERAL, (i) of a large body of people; 2. 3. 59; (ii) common to a whole class or sex; 2. 3. 183

GET, beget; 4. 2. 90

GIDDY, fickle; 4. 4. 88; 5. 2. 78

GILT, gilded (p. tense of 'gild'); 2. 1. 6

GLOZE, use fair (but specious) words; 4. 4. 35

GODDEN, good evening; 4. 4. 44

GOLDEN, auspicious, happy, refreshing; 2. 3. 26 (cf. note); 4. 4. 98

GOVERN, direct, carry through (a plan); 5. 2. 139

GRACE (vb.), (i) show favour to; 2. 1. 27; (ii) adorn, embellish; 5. 2. 17

GRACIOUS, (i) finding favour, acceptable; 1. 1. 11, 170, 429; 2. 1. 32; (ii) bestowing favour, merciful, favourable; 1. 1. 60, 78, 104; 3. 1. 157; 5. 3. 96

GRAMERCY (fr. 'grand merci'), great thanks; 1. 1. 495; 4. 2. 7

GRATIFY, reward; 1. 1. 220; 4. 2. 12

GRATULATE, show joy at; 1. 1. 221

GRIEF, sense of grievance; 1. 1 438, 443

GROOM, fellow; 4. 2. 165

GROUND, (a) foundation, basis; (b) (in music) bass or plain-song to a descant; 2. 1. 70

HAND (OUT OF), on the spur of the moment; 5. 2. 77

HANDSOMELY, handily, conveniently; 2. 3. 268

HEAD, armed force; 4. 4. 64

HEAVINESS, sorrow; 3. 2. 49

HEAVY, sorrowful; 3. 1. 277; 4. 3. 25; 5. 2. 24; 5. 3. 150

HECUBA, Queen of Troy, wife of Priam (v. Ham. 2. 2. 505 ff.); 4. 1. 20

HIGH-WITTED, supremely cunning; 4. 4. 35

HIT IT, (a) find the right solution (not pre-Shn.); (b) in an equivocal sense (v. G. L.L.L.); 2. 1. 97

HOLD! here! (when proffering a tip); 4. 3. 104

HONESTY, chastity; 2. 3. 135

HONEY-DEW, 'sweet, sticky substance, found on leaves and stems of plants' (O.E.D.); 3. 1. 112

HONEY-STALKS, stalks of clover flowers. App. a coinage by Sh. (v. note). '"Honey-suckle" was anciently a name for red clover, and is still in Warwickshire and other midland districts' (Onions); 4. 4. 92

HOPEFUL, hoped for; 2. 3. 49

HORN (vb.), cuckold a husband; 2. 3. 67

HUE, appearance, style of beauty; 1. 1. 261

HUMBLE (vb.), (i) subject, submit; 1. 1. 51; (ii) offer humbly; 1. 1. 252; (iii) make humble; 1. 1. 472

HUMOUR, caprice; 4. 3. 29;
4. 4. 19; 5. 2. 140

HYMENÆUS, Hymen, god of
marriage, here = the mar-
riage ceremony; 1. 1. 325

HYPERION, the sun-god, the
sun; 5. 2. 56

IGNOMY, ignominy (freq. 16th-
and 17th-c. form); 4. 2. 115

IMPERIOUS, (i) imperial; 1. 1.
250; 4. 4. 82; (ii) com-
manding; 5. 1. 6

IMPIETY, lack of natural 'piety'
(q.v.); 1. 1. 355

INCREASE, offspring (freq. in
Sh.); 5. 2. 192

INDIFFERENTLY, impartially, as
a neutral; 1. 1. 430

INGRATEFUL, ungrateful. The
commonest form in Sh.;
5. 1. 12

INHERIT, enjoy possession of
(comm. sense in Sh.); 2. 3. 3

INSINUATE, curry favour (cf.
Ric. II, 4. 1. 165); 4. 2.
38

INSULT ON, triumph scornfully
over; 3. 2. 71

INTERCEPT, interrupt; 3. 1. 40

INTEREST (sb.), claim or title to
enjoy possession, hence, en-
joyment; 3. 1. 250

JAR (vb.), lit. make musical
discord, (hence) disagree;
2. 1. 103

JET, encroach; 2. 1. 64

JOY (vb.), enjoy; 2. 3. 83

JUST (adv.), exactly; 4. 2. 24

KEEP, (i) hold, defend; 1. 1. 12;
(ii) keep on making; 4. 2. 57;
(iii) remain in; 5. 2. 5

KILL (one's heart); break (cf.
Hen. V, 2. 1. 87); 3. 2. 54

KIND, nature (of the thing mentioned); 2. 1. 116; 2. 3. 281

KIND (adj.), filial, loving; 1. 1. 61

KNIT, (i) tie; 2. 4. 10; (ii)
unite; 5. 3. 70

LADING, cargo; 1. 1. 72

LAMENTING, lamentable; 3. 2.
62

LANGUISHMENT, pining for
love, lovesickness (cf. Lucr
l. 1141; elsewhere in Sh.
'languishing'; 2. 1. 110

LANGUOR, affliction, sorrow,
mourning. Mod. sense not
found before 1650; 3. 1. 13

LATEST, last; 1. 1. 83, 149;
5. 3. 169

LEAGUE, amity (cf. Ric. III,
1. 3. 281; John, 2. 1. 417);
5. 3. 23

LEAN, bare (cf. 1 Hen. IV,
1. 2. 72, 'lean wardrobe');
2. 3. 94

LEAVE, leave off; 1. 1. 424

LEER, countenance, com-
plexion (cf. A.Y.L.I. 4. 1.
64); 4. 2. 119

LEISURE, (BY), very slowly, i.e.
not at all; 1. 1. 301

LESSON (vb.), teach; 5. 2. 110

LET ALONE, trust (cf. Tw. Nt
3. 4. 187); 4. 3. 113

LIBEL (vb. intr.), publish libels;
4. 4. 17

LIMBO. Properly, an abode on
edge of Hell (v. note); 3. 1.
149

LIVELY, (i) living; 3. 1. 105;
(ii) striking; 5. 3. 44

LOOK BACK, relent; 1. 1. 481

LOVE-DAY, (a) lit. day appointed for a meeting to
settle a dispute; (b) quib-
bling: a day given up to love
(v. note); 1. 1. 491

Lustily, merrily (cf. *A.Y.L.I.* 4. 2. 18); 2. 2. 14

Luxurious, lascivious; 5. 1. 88

Mad (vb.), madden; 3. 1. 104

Make away, kill; 2. 3. 189, 208; 4. 2. 168

Manes, spirits of the dead; 1. 1. 98

Map, picture (cf. *Ric. II*, 5. 1. 12); 3. 2. 12

Mark, (i) (mark to), mark out (for); 1. 1. 125

Marked, branded (cf. *K. John*, 4. 2. 221); 4. 2. 9

Martyr (vb.), (i) mutilate, disfigure (cf. *Lucr.* l. 802); 3. 1. 81, 107; (ii) kill; 5. 2. 181

Martyred, belonging to a martyr; 3. 2. 36

Maugre, in spite of; 4. 2. 110

May, can; 1. 1. 475; 2. 1. 107; 2. 4. 20; 4. 3. 29

Mean (sb.); means; 2. 4. 40

Meaner, humbler, of lower rank; 2. 1. 73

Melting, (a) (lit.) dissolving in rain; (b) (fig.) yielding to tender emotion; 3. 1. 214

Mesh, or (mash) lit. 'mix (malt) with hot water to form wort' (O.E.D.); here, brew; 3. 2. 38

Message, errand (sense in Sh., as still in Scotland); 4. 1. 118

Minion, jade, hussy; 2. 3. 124

Mischief (stronger sense than mod.), calamity; 5. 1. 65

Mo, more (in number); 5. 3. 17

Motion, proposal; 1. 1. 243

Mutiny, rebellion; 4. 1. 86

Mutual, common; 5. 3. 71, 134

Napkin, handkerchief; 3. 1. 140, 146

Nature, natural affection; 1. 1. 370, 371; 5. 3. 150

Nice-preserved, preserved by coyness; 2. 3. 135

Nip, (a) afflict; (b) freeze; 4. 4. 71

Noise, music; 2. 2. 6

Note, stigmatize, defame (cf. *Caes.* 4. 3. 2); 2. 3. 86

Nourish, nurse; 5. 1. 60, 84

Object, spectacle. Lit. something presented to the sight; 3. 1. 64

Obsequious, of dutiful sorrow. (The mod. pejorative sense not in Sh.); 5. 3. 152

O'ercome (p. part.), overrun, overgrown; 2. 3. 95

Officious, zealous in performing a duty; 5. 2. 202

Onset, beginning, first step (cf. *Gent.* 3. 2. 94); 1. 1. 238

Opinion, reputation, credit; 1. 1. 416

Oppose, compare (Lat. *opponere*); 1. 1. 132

Ordain, design, plan; 5. 3. 22

Out, interj. of horror, sorrow, indignation, etc.; 'out alas!' (cf. *Son.* 33. 11); 2. 3. 258; 'out on thee!'; 3. 2. 54

Outrageous, very violent, furious; 3. 2. 13

Overbear, treat insolently; 4. 4. 2

Overlook, look down on from above (freq. in Sh.); 2. 1. 8

Overshine, outshine; 1. 1. 317

Overween, be presumptuous; 2. 1. 29

Pack (vb.), plot, conspire; 4. 2. 156

PAINS, birth-pains; 4. 2. 47

PAINTED, specious, unreal (cf. *A.Y.L.I.* 2. 1. 3); 2. 3. 126

PALLIAMENT, candidate's white gown (v. *candidatus*). Only found here and in Peele's *Honour of the Garter*, ll. 91, 92; coinage from either *pallium* = cloak, or *paludamentum* = military cloak; 1. 1. 182

PANTHEON, building in Rome, erected 27 B.C., adorned with statues of many gods (hence the name = 'of all the gods'); here, as commonly, supposed to be a temple to all the gods; consecrated as a Christian church by Boniface IV; 1. 1. 242, 333

PARCEL, small party or company of persons; 2. 3. 49

PART (sb.), 'in p. of' = in recognition of, extension of sense 'on behalf of'; 1. 1. 236

PART (vb.), depart; 1. 1. 488

PARTY, representative; 1. 1. 21

PASSION, powerful emotion, e.g. grief; 1. 1. 106; 3. 1. 218; 3. 2. 48

PASSIONATE (vb.), passionately express (cf. *F.Q.* 1. 12. 16; here only in Sh.); 3. 2. 6

PATIENCE, indulgence; 2. 3. 66

PATIENT (oneself), be patient; 1. 1. 121

PATTERN (vb.), provide with a pattern or precedent; 4. 1. 58

PEER (vb.), come in sight, appear ('highest-peering' = showing up above all others); 2. 1. 8

PERFECT (adj.), 'to be perfect in' = to know by heart; 3. 2. 40

PHILOMEL (or PHILOMELA), Athenian maiden, outraged by her brother-in-law Tereus, who afterwards cut out her tongue to prevent disclosure; 2. 3. 43; 2. 4. 38, 43; 4. 1. 48, 53; 5. 2. 195

PHOEBE, Diana; 1. 1. 316

PIECE, contemptuous term for a woman, 'creature', 'thing'; 1. 1. 309

PIETY (Lat. *pietas*; cf. Virgil's '*pius Aeneas*'), right conduct towards the gods, the state, or the family; 1. 1. 115

PIPE (for) (vb.), whistle, call in vain (for); 4. 3. 24

PITCH (term of falconry), highest point (to wh. a hawk soars) (cf. *Ric. III*, 3. 7. 188; *Ham.* 3. 1. 86); 2. 1. 14

PLAIN, level; 4. 1. 70

PLAY A PRIZE, engage in a contest or match (often contemptuous); 1. 1. 399

PLEDGE (sb.), (i) bail, surety; 4. 4. 107; 5. 1. 163; (ii) i.e. parent or child (pledge of love; cf. Lat. *pignus*); 3. 1. 292

PLOT (sb.), spot, piece of ground; 4. 1. 70

PLUTO, sovereign god of Hades; 4. 3. 13, 37

POLICY, craft, crafty device; 2. 1. 104; 4. 2. 149

POWER, (i) heavenly being; 3. 1. 209; (ii) army; 3. 1. 300; 4. 4. 64

PRACTICE, scheme; 5. 2. 77

PRESENT, immediate; 2. 3. 173

PRESENTLY, immediately; 2. 3. 62; 4. 2. 167; 4. 4. 46; 5. 1. 146; 5. 3. 59

PRETEND, profess; 1. 1. 42

PRIVILEGE, immunity cf. (*Ric. III*, 3. 1. 41); 4. 4. 58

PRODIGIES, ominous events, 1. 1. 101

PROGNE, sister of Philomela (v. *Philomel*), in revenge for whose violation she killed her son Itys, and gave his flesh for her husband, Tereus, to eat; 5. 2. 196

PROPORTION, shape, form (cf. *Merch*, 3. 4. 14); 5. 2. 106

PROPOSE, i.e. to carry out (Lat. *proponere*); 2. 1. 80

PROUD, spirited, fierce, cruel; 2. 2. 21; 3. 1. 291; 4. 4. 26, 59

PURCHASE, obtain, win; 2. 3. 275

PUT TO, bring to, cause to come to; 5. 3. 150

PUT UP, put up with; 1. 1. 433

PYRAMUS, lover of Thisbe, who, finding her veil covered with blood, supposed her slain, and killed himself; whereafter she finding him dead killed herself likewise (v. Ovid, *Metam.* IV, and *M.N.D.* 5. 1); 2. 3. 231

QUESTION, talk to, discuss with; 2. 3. 48

QUIT, requite, pay back; 1. 1. 141

QUOTE, mark, observe, distinguish (cf. *Rom.* 1. 4. 31, etc.); 4. 1. 51

RAGGED, rugged, irregular, broken (cf. *Gent.* 1. 2. 121); 2. 3. 230

RAPINE, rape; 5. 2. 59, 62, 83, 103

RECEPTACLE, sepulchre, vault. Cf. *Rom.* 4. 3. 39. Lit. a place for retirement or security, room, apartment (O.E.D. 2); 1. 1. 92; 2. 3. 235

REFLECT, shine (cf. *Ric. III*, 1. 4. 31; *Lucr.* l. 376); 1. 1. 226

RESERVE, preserve; 1. 1. 165

RESOLVE, answer (a question), solve (a problem); 5. 3. 35

RESOLVED, resolute (in face of some evil) (cf. *Meas.* 3. 2. 240—'resolved to die'); 1. 1. 135

REST (sb.), restoration to strength (cf. *1 Hen. IV*, 4. 3. 27); 4. 2. 63

REST (vb.), rely; 1. 1. 267; ('rest in'), depend (on); 2. 3. 41

ROSED, rosy; 2. 4. 24

ROUND ABOUT, all over, everywhere; 4. 2. 18; 5. 2. 98

ROUSE, make rise from lair (technical hunting term); 2. 2. 21

RUDE-GROWING, rough; 2. 3. 199

RUFFLE, swagger, bully; 1. 1. 313

SAD, dismal (cf. *Ric. II*, 5. 5. 70); 5. 2. 11

SANGUINE, ruddy, red-faced; 4. 2. 97

SAUCINESS, insolence (stronger than the mod. word); 2. 3. 82

SAUCY, insolent; 2. 3. 60

SCATH, harm (cf. *2 Hen. VI*, 2. 4. 62; *Ric. III*, 1. 3. 317; *K. John*, 2. 1. 75); 5. 1. 7

SCROWL (vb.). 'A form of "scrawl"', gesticulate, 'with a play on "scroll", to write down' (Onions); 2. 4. 5

SEAL, token; 4. 2. 69

SEARCH, probe (a wound); 2. 3. 262

SECURE (of), safe (from); 2. 1. 3

SELF, same (cf. *3 Hen. VI*, 3. 1. 11; *Merch.* 1. 1. 148); 4. 2. 123

SEMIRAMIS, mythical Assyrian queen, wife of Ninus, proverbial for sexual licence; 2. 1. 22; 2. 3. 118

SENSIBLY. Meaning doubtful: (either) as regards the bodily faculties; (or), as common sense tells us, plainly; 4. 2. 122

SEQUESTER, separate; 2. 3. 75

SERVE, ('serve one's turn'), satisfy one (sexually; cf. *L.L.L.* 1. 1. 289); 2. 1. 96

SET (abroad), set on foot, stir up; 1. 1. 192

SHAPE, create, fashion; 4. 4. 58

SHIFT, contrivance, trick; 4. 1. 73; 4. 2. 177

SHIVE, slice (only here in Sh.); 2. 1. 87

SHORT, rude; 1. 1. 409

SHRINK, shrivel up, wither away; 3. 1. 248

SIBYL, generic name of ancient Italian prophetesses, e.g. the Cumaean Sibyl, who wrote prophetic answers to inquiries on leaves, and placed them outside her cave, where the wind blew them away unless they were collected quickly; 4. 1. 106

SINGLE (vb. tr.) separate, single out. A hunting term = select one from the herd (v. note, and Madden, p. 31 n., citing Turbervile, *Booke of Hunting*, 1576—Tudor and Stuart Library, p. 244); 2. 1. 117; 2. 3. 69

SINK (sb.), sewer, cesspool (cf. *Troil.* 5. 1. 83; *Cor.* 1. 1. 126); 3. 2. 19

SINON, Greek who as pretended deserter persuaded the Trojans to admit the wooden horse to Troy; 5. 3. 85

SLAUGHTER-MAN, slayer (v. note); 4. 4. 59

SLIP (sb.), (i) offence, fault (cf. *Ham.* 2. 1. 22); 2. 3. 86; (ii) scion; 5. 1. 9

SMELL (of), smack (of); 2. 1. 132

SMOOTH (vb.), soothe, flatter; 4. 4. 97; 5. 2. 140

SMOKE FOR IT, suffer for it. Orig. burn as a heretic for it. Mod. 'get it hot'; 4. 2. 111

SNATCH (sb.), swift catch (equivocal; v. O.E.D. 6*b*); 2. 1. 95

SOLEMN, grand, ceremonious, formal; 2. 1. 112; 5. 2. 115

SOLON, statesman of Athens (c. 640–558 B.C.), famed for his new constitution of Athens (c. 594); 1. 1. 177

SPEED, (i) fare well (v. note); 1. 1. 372; (ii) succeed; 2. 1. 101

SPLEENFUL, passionate, lustful (cf. *Troil.* 2. 2. 196); 2. 3. 191

SPOIL (sb.), spoliation; 4. 4. 65

SPOTTED, stained, polluted (cf. *Ric. II*, 3. 2. 134; *M.N.D.* 1. 1. 110; *Lear*, 5. 3. 138); 2. 3. 74

SPRAWL, struggle in death-agony; 5. 1. 51

SPURN (sb.), lit. contemptuous thrust; 3. 1. 101

SQUARE (vb.), (i) (intr.), quarrel (cf. *M.N.D.* 2. 1. 30); 2. 1. 100; (ii) (refl.), quarrel (or perh., settle matters with each other); 2. 1. 124; (iii) (tr.), shape, frame (cf. *Meas.* 5. 1. 478); 3. 2. 31

STAIN (vb.), make dim, eclipse (freq. in Sh.); 3. 1. 213

STALE (sb.), dupe, laughing-stock (cf. *3 Hen. VI*, 3. 3. 260); 1. 1. 304

STAMP, lit. coin; hence, thing stamped with a certain impression; 4. 2. 69

STANCH, satiate; 3. 1. 14

STAND ON, insist upon; 4. 4. 106

STAND UPON, rely upon; 2. 3. 124

STARVED, numb with cold; 3. 1. 252

STERN, cruel; 2. 4. 16; 5. 2. 204

STINT (vb.), make cease (cf. *Hen. VIII*, 1. 2. 76); 4. 4. 87

STOP, close up; 2. 4. 36

STORE, treasury; 1. 1. 94

STRIKE, (i) (*a*) strike down a quarry with spear or arrow, (*b*) sense (ii); 2. 1. 118; (ii) obscene sense; 2. 1. 129; (iii) 'strike down' = destroy by malign influence (astrological term); 2. 4. 14

STUPRUM (Lat.), rape; 4. 1. 79

SUBTLE, (i) cunning, crafty; 1. 1. 392; 5. 3. 84; (ii) treacherous; 2. 3. 198

SUCCESSANTLY. Meaning doubtful (v. Introd. p. lvi). O.E.D. gives no other example, and glosses: 'Arbitrarily from L. *success—succēdĕre*, to succeed, + ant + ly. ?' In succession'; 4. 4. 114

SUCCESSIVE (title), (title) to the succession; 1. 1. 4

SUPPOSE (sb.), supposition (cf. *Shrew*, 5. 1. 113); 1. 1. 440

SURANCE, assurance (here only in Sh.); 5. 2. 46

SURE, (i) certain; 2. 3. 133; (ii) harmless, (cf. *1 Hen. IV*, 5. 4. 125); 2. 3. 187 (here = dead); 5. 2. 76

SURE CARD, 'an expedient certain to attain its object', a person by whose agency success is assured (O.E.D.); 5. 1. 100

SURPRISE, dumbfound, bewilder (cf. *V.A.* l. 890); 2. 3. 211

SUUM CUIQUE, to each his own (Lat.); 1. 1. 280

SWEET, perfumed; 2. 4. 6

SWELL, overflow; 1. 1. 153; 5. 3. 13

SWELLING, swollen (with venom); 2. 3. 101

SWOUND, swoon; 5. 1. 119

TAKE, suppose (mod. 'take to be'); 5. 2. 154

TAKE UP, settle amicably, make friends with (cf. *A.Y.L.* 5. 4. 47, 96); 1. 1. 457; 4. 3. 92

TEDIOUS, laboriously executed; 2. 4. 39

TEMPER, (i) work upon; 4. 4. 110; (ii) mix with a fluid; 5. 2. 200

TENDER (vb.), have a tender regard for (cf. *Ham.* 1. 3. 107); 1. 1. 476

TEREUS, brother-in-law and violator of Philomela (v. *Philomel*); 2. 4. 26, 41; 4. 1. 49

GLOSSARY

THROW DOWN, overthrow; 3. 1. 164

TICE, entice (here only in Sh.); 2. 3. 92

TIMELESS, untimely (cf. *Gent.* 3. 1. 21); 2. 3. 265

TITAN, god of the sun, the sun (cf. *1 Hen. IV*, 2 4. 116); 1. 1. 226; 2. 4. 31

TOFORE, hitherto, previously (cf. *L.L.L.* 3. 1. 82); 3. 1. 294

TOSS, turn over the leaves of (a book); 4. 1. 41

TOUCH (vb.), wound, hurt (cf. *Cymb.* 4. 3. 4); 4. 4. 36

TRAIN (vb.), lure (cf. *Err.* 3. 2. 45, etc.); 5. 1. 104

TRIBUNAL PLEBS, clown's error for *tribunus plebis*, tribune of the plebs; 4. 3. 92

TRIUMPHER, general awarded a 'triumph' in Rome; 1. 1. 170

TROPHY, emblem or memorial placed on a tomb; 1. 1. 388

TRULL, prostitute; 2. 3. 191

TRUST, trusted person (cf. *1 Hen. VI*, 4. 4. 20); 1. 1. 181

TULLY, Cicero, the Roman statesman and orator; 4. 1. 14

TURN (sb.), (*a*) purpose, requirement; (*b*) action performed in rotation, taken in turn; 2. 1. 96

TURN (vb.), return; 5. 2. 141

TWENTY, indef. for a large number; 5. 1. 76, 120

TYPHON, father of the Titans (v. *Enceladus*); 4. 2. 94

TYRANNY, cruelty; 2. 3. 145

UNADVISED, ill-advisedly, unwisely; 2. 1. 38

UNCOUTH, strange, uncanny; 2. 3. 211

UNDO, (*a*) ruin; 4. 2. 55, 75, 77; (*b*) annul; 4. 2. 74

UNFURNISHED, lit. unequipped, unaccompanied; 2. 3. 56

UNKIND(LY), (*a*) cruel(ly); (*b*) unnatural(ly); 5. 3. 48, 104

UNRECURING, incurable; 3. 1. 90

UNREST, indisposition; 4. 2. 31

UP AND DOWN, altogether (cf. *Gent.* 2. 3. 28–9; *Ado*, 2. 1. 107–8); 5. 2. 107

URCHIN, hedgehog (gen. assoc. with witchcraft or devils; cf. *Macb.* 4. 1. 2; *Temp.* 1. 2. 327); 2. 3. 101

URGE, mention, insist upon; 3. 2. 26

URN, water-jug (O.E.D. 4); 3. 1. 17

VARY (music), repeat the same theme with modifications; 3. 1. 86

VAST, desolate; 4. 1. 54, 5. 2. 36

VENEREAL, erotic (cf. Nashe, McKerrow, i. 19; ii. 271); 2. 3. 37

VOICE, vote; 1. 1. 218, 230

VOUCH, maintain (here, by force of arms); 1. 1. 360

VULCAN, the husband of Venus, cuckolded by Mars; 2. 1. 89

WAG, move about, go on one's way; 5. 2. 87

WAGGON, chariot; 5. 2. 51, 54

WAGGONER, charioteer; 5. 2. 48

WAIT (on), attend to, obey; 4. 1. 123

WALL-EYED, glaring, fierce (lit. having the iris of the eye discoloured, which gives a look of fierceness); 5. 1. 44

WASTED (of a building), ruined (cf. *1 Hen. VI*, 3. 3. 46; *Son.* 125. 4); 5. 1. 23

WATCH, stay awake; 3. 1. 5

WELL-ADVISED, in one's right mind; 4. 2. 10

WELL-BESEEMING, well-becoming; 2. 3. 56

WELL SAID! well done! 4. 3. 63

WHAT (interrog.), why; 1. 1. 189

WHEAK, squeak (v. note); 4. 2. 146

WHITE-LIMED, whitewashed (v. note); 4. 2. 98

WILDERNESS. Sh. thought of a wilderness or desert chiefly as a place where neither law nor mercy held sway; cf. *Lucr.* l. 544, 'Pleads, in a wilderness where are no laws, To the rough beast'; 3. 1. 54, 94

WIND (vb.), scent (v. note); 4. 1. 98

WIND (sb.), windward side ('have the w. of' = keep a watch on, like a hunter following game down the wind); 4. 2. 133

WINK, shut the eyes; 3. 2. 43

WIT, wisdom, intelligence; 2. 1. 10, 26, 120; 2. 3. 1

WITTY, wise, clever; 4. 2. 29

WORLDLY, of this world; 5. 2. 65

WRIT, writing; 2. 3. 264

YELLOW. Apparently an extension of 'yell', on the analogy of 'bellow' (O.E.D.); 2. 3. 20

YOKE (sb.), (i) submission; 1. 1. 69; (ii) sovereignty, government; 1. 1. 111; 4. 1. 110

YOKE (vb.), subdue, bring under the yoke; 1. 1. 30

YOUNGLING (contemptuous), youngster, novice (cf. *Shrew*, 2. 1. 330); 2. 1. 73; 4. 2. 93

ZOUNDS, an oath = God's wounds (cf. *K. John*, 2. 1. 466); 4. 2. 71

WORDSWORTH CLASSICS

General Editors: Marcus Clapham & Clive Reynard

JANE AUSTEN
Emma
Mansfield Park
Northanger Abbey
Persuasion
Pride and Prejudice
Sense and Sensibility

ARNOLD BENNETT
Anna of the Five Towns

R. D. BLACKMORE
Lorna Doone

ANNE BRONTË
Agnes Grey
The Tenant of
Wildfell Hall

CHARLOTTE BRONTË
Jane Eyre
The Professor
Shirley
Villette

EMILY BRONTË
Wuthering Heights

JOHN BUCHAN
Greenmantle
Mr Standfast
The Thirty-Nine Steps

SAMUEL BUTLER
The Way of All Flesh

LEWIS CARROLL
Alice in Wonderland

CERVANTES
Don Quixote

G. K. CHESTERTON
Father Brown:
Selected Stories
The Man who was
Thursday

ERSKINE CHILDERS
The Riddle of the Sands

JOHN CLELAND
Memoirs of a Woman of
Pleasure: Fanny Hill

WILKIE COLLINS
The Moonstone
The Woman in White

JOSEPH CONRAD
Heart of Darkness
Lord Jim
The Secret Agent

J. FENIMORE COOPER
The Last of the
Mohicans

STEPHEN CRANE
The Red Badge of
Courage

THOMAS DE QUINCEY
Confessions of an English
Opium Eater

DANIEL DEFOE
Moll Flanders
Robinson Crusoe

CHARLES DICKENS
Bleak House
David Copperfield
Great Expectations
Hard Times
Little Dorrit
Martin Chuzzlewit
Oliver Twist
Pickwick Papers
A Tale of Two Cities

BENJAMIN DISRAELI
Sybil

THEODOR DOSTOEVSKY
Crime and Punishment

SIR ARTHUR CONAN
DOYLE
The Adventures of
Sherlock Holmes
The Case-Book of
Sherlock Holmes
The Lost World &
Other Stories
The Return of
Sherlock Holmes
Sir Nigel

GEORGE DU MAURIER
Trilby

ALEXANDRE DUMAS
The Three Musketeers

MARIA EDGEWORTH
Castle Rackrent

GEORGE ELIOT
The Mill on the Floss
Middlemarch
Silas Marner

HENRY FIELDING
Tom Jones

F. SCOTT FITZGERALD
A Diamond as Big as the
Ritz & Other Stories
The Great Gatsby
Tender is the Night

GUSTAVE FLAUBERT
Madame Bovary

JOHN GALSWORTHY
In Chancery
The Man of Property
To Let

ELIZABETH GASKELL
Cranford
North and South

KENNETH GRAHAME
The Wind in the
Willows

GEORGE & WEEDON
GROSSMITH
Diary of a Nobody

RIDER HAGGARD
She

THOMAS HARDY
Far from the
Madding Crowd
The Mayor of Casterbridge
The Return of the
Native
Tess of the d'Urbervilles
The Trumpet Major
Under the Greenwood
Tree

DISTRIBUTION

**AUSTRALIA
& PAPUA NEW GUINEA**
Peribo Pty Ltd
58 Beaumont Road, Mount Kuring-Gai
NSW 2080, Australia
Tel: (02) 457 0011 Fax: (02) 457 0022

CYPRUS
Huckleberry Trading
3 Othos Avvey, Tala Paphos
Tel: 06 653585

CZECH REPUBLIC
Bohemian Ventures spol s r o
Delnicka 13, 170 00 Prague 7
Tel: 02 877837 Fax: 02 801498

FRANCE
Copernicus Diffusion
23 Rue Saint Dominique, Paris 75007
Tel: 1 44 11 33 20 Fax: 1 44 11 33 21

GERMANY
**GLBmbH (Bargain, Promotional
& Remainder Shops)**
Schönhauser Strasse 25
D-50968 Köln
Tel: 0221 34 20 92 Fax: 0221 38 40 40

**Tradis Verlag und Vertrieb GmbH
(Bookshops)**
Postfach 90 03 69
D-51113 Köln
Tel: 022 03 31059
Fax: 022 03 3 93 40

GREAT BRITAIN & IRELAND
Wordsworth Editions Ltd
Cumberland House, Crib Street
Ware, Hertfordshire SG12 9ET

INDIA
OM Book Service
1690 First Floor
Nai Sarak, Delhi – 110006
Tel: 3279823-3265303 Fax: 3278091

ISRAEL
Timmy Marketing Limited
Israel Ben Zeev 12
Ramont Gimmel, Jerusalem
Tel: 02-865266 Fax: 02-880035

ITALY
Magis Books SRL
Via Raffaello 31/C
Zona Ind Mancasale
42100 Reggio Emilia
Tel: 1522 920999 Fax: 0522 920666

NEW ZEALAND & FIJI
Allphy Book Distributors Ltd
4-6 Charles Street, Eden Terrace
Auckland,
Tel: (09) 3773096 Fax: (09) 3022770

NORTH AMERICA
Universal Sales & Marketing
230 Fifth Avenue, Suite 1212
New York, NY 10001, USA
Tel: 212 481 3500 Fax: 212 481 3534

PHILIPPINES
I J Sagun Enterprises
P O Box 4322 CPO Manila
2 Topaz Road, Greenheights Village
Taytay, Rizal
Tel: 631 80 61 TO 66

PORTUGAL
International Publishing Services Ltd
Rua da Cruz da Carreira, 4B,
1100 Lisbon
Tel: 01 570051 Fax: 01 3522066

**SOUTHERN, CENTRAL
& EAST AFRICA**
**P.M.C.International Importers &
Exporters CC**
Unit 6, Ben-Sarah Place, 52-56 Columbina
Place, Glen Anil, Kwa-Zulu Natal 4051
P.O.Box 201520
Durban North, Kwa-Zulu Natal 4016
Tel: (031) 844441 Fax: (031) 844466

SCOTLAND
Lomond Books
36 West Shore Road, Granton
Edinburgh EH5 1QD

**SINGAPORE,
MALASIA & BRUNEI**
Paul & Elizabeth Book Services Pte Ltd
163 Tanglin Road No 03-15/16
Tanglin Mall, Singapore 1024
Tel: (65) 735 7308 Fax: (65) 735 9747

SLOVAK REPUBLIC
Slovak Ventures spol s r o
Stefanikova 128, 94901 Nitra
Tel/Fax: 087 25105

SPAIN
Ribera Libros, S.L.
Poligono Martiartu, Calle 1 - no 6
48480 Arrigorriaga, Vizcaya
Tel: 34 4 6713607 (Almacen)
      34 4 4418787 (Libreria)
Fax: 34 4 6713608 (Almacen)
      34 4 4418029 (Libreria)